Answer Key

to Introduction to Biblical Hebrew

ANSWER KEY

TO

INTRODUCTION TO BIBLICAL HEBREW

SECOND EDITION

Lee Roy Martin

CPT Press
Cleveland, Tennessee USA

ANSWER KEY TO INTRODUCTION TO BIBLICAL HEBREW

Second Edition

Published by CPT Press
900 Walker ST NE
Cleveland, TN 37311
email: cptpress@pentecostaltheology.org
website: www.pentecostaltheology.org

ISBN-13: 978-1-935931-75-1

Preface

This answer key supplies all of the answers to the exercises in Lee Roy Martin's *Introduction to Biblical Hebrew* (Fourth Edition), published by CPT Press, Cleveland, TN 2018, ISBN-13: 978-1-935931-74-4.

In addition to the answers, a copy of all of the exercises themselves is included here.

CHAPTER 1

Most of the exercises in chapter one involve oral recitation. The following pages, however, will provide space for the practice of your writing skills.

Begin by tracing over the Hebrew Letters. Observe that Hebrew is written from right to left, and letters are written from the top line downward. After you have finished the tracing, you should continue to practice writing the letter until you can write it comfortably. Try to draw the letters the same size as the examples. As you write each letter, you should say its name and its pronunciation.

The first letter is *alef*, and it is silent.

The next letter is *beyt*, and it sounds like the *b* in *boy*.

2

ג The next letter is *gimel*, and it sounds like the *g* in *good*.

ד The next letter is *dalet*, and it sounds like the *d* in *dog*.

ה

The next letter is *heh*, and it sounds like the *h* in *how*.

ו

The next letter is *vav*, and it sounds like the *v* in *vet*.

4

ז   The next letter is *zayin*, and it sounds like the *z* in *zoo*.

ח   The next letter is *chet*, and it sounds like the *ch* in *loch*.

The next letter is *tet*, and it sounds like the *t* in *toy*.

The next letter is *yod*, and it sounds like the *y* in *yard*.

6

The next letter is *kaf*, and it sounds like the *k* in *kitchen*.

The next letter is *final Kaf*, and it sounds like the *ch* in *loch*.

ל The next letter is *lamed*, and it sounds like the *l* in *life*.

מ The next letter is *mem*, and it sounds like the *m* in *man*.

ם   The next letter is *final mem*, and it sounds like the *m* in *man*.

נ   The next letter is *nun*, and it sounds like the *n* in *next*.

ן The next letter is *final nun*, and it sounds like the *n* in *next*.

ן

ס The next letter is *samek*, and it sounds like the *s* in *see*.

ס

ע The next letter is *ayin*, which is silent.

פ The next letter is *peh*, and it sounds like the *p* in *pen*.

ף The next letter is *final peh*, and it sounds like the *ph* in *phone*.

צ The next letter is *tsade*, and it sounds like the *ts* in *cats*.

12

ץ The next letter is *final tsade*, and it sounds like the *ts* in *cats*.

ק The next letter is *qof*, and it sounds like the *q* in *queen*.

ר The next letter is *resh*, and it sounds like the *r* in *run*.

ש The next letter is *seen*, and it sounds like the *s* in *see*.

14

שׁ The next letter is *sheen*, and it sounds like the *sh* in *shine*.

ת The next letter is *tav*, and it sounds like the *t* in *time*.

The following Hebrew Scripture (Zeph. 3.8) is the only verse in the Bible that contains all the shapes of the alphabet, including all five of the final forms (Remember that *seen* and *sheen* have the same shape, only the dot is placed differently). Copy the verse in the blank space below.

לָכֵן חַכּוּ־לִי נְאֻם־יְהוָה לְיוֹם קוּמִי לְעַד

כִּי מִשְׁפָּטִי לֶאֱסֹף גּוֹיִם לְקָבְצִי מַמְלָכוֹת

לִשְׁפֹּךְ עֲלֵיהֶם זַעְמִי כֹּל חֲרוֹן אַפִּי

כִּי בְּאֵשׁ קִנְאָתִי תֵּאָכֵל כָּל־הָאָרֶץ

CHAPTER 2

Exercise 2-A

Form the plural of the following masculine words.

דָּבָר	word, thing	דְּבָרִים	הַר	mountain	הָרִים
יוֹם	day	יָמִים	אִישׁ	man	אֲנָשִׁים
מִקְדָּשׁ	sanctuary	מִקְדָּשִׁים	מִשְׁפָּט	judgment	מִשְׁפָּטִים
נָבִיא	prophet	נְבִיאִים	אָב	father	אָבוֹת

Exercise 2-B

PART 1: Add the definite article to the following Hebrew words.

דֶּרֶךְ	road, way	הַדֶּרֶךְ
חַי	life, living	הַחַי
יָד	hand	הַיָּד
יוֹם	day	הַיּוֹם
כֹּהֵן	priest	הַכֹּהֵן
לֵב	heart	הַלֵּב
יָם	sea	הַיָּם
מֶלֶךְ	king	הַמֶּלֶךְ
נֶפֶשׁ	soul, life	הַנֶּפֶשׁ
מַיִם	water	הַמַּיִם

Exercise 2-B

PART 2: Translate the following English words into Hebrew:

the brother	הָאָח
the husband	הָאִישׁ
the father	הָאָב
the son	הַבֵּן
the daughter	הַבַּת
the God	הָאֱלֹהִים
the house	הַבַּיִת
the women	הַנָּשִׁים
the sons	הַבָּנִים
the fathers	הָאָבוֹת
the words	הַדְּבָרִים

CHAPTER 3

Exercise 3-A

Part 1: Translate the following Hebrew into English:

1.	הָאִשָּׁה הַטּוֹבָה	the good woman
2.	הַסּוּסוֹת טוֹבוֹת	The mares are good.
3.	מְלָכוֹת טוֹבוֹת	good queens
4.	אָח טוֹב	a good brother
5.	הַבֵּן טוֹב	The son is good.
6.	הַמְּלָכוֹת הַטּוֹבוֹת	the good queens
7.	הַדָּבָר הַטּוֹב	the good word
8.	הַמְּלָכִים הַטּוֹבִים	the good kings
9.	טוֹבָה הָאָרֶץ	Numbers 14.7 The land is good
10.	טוֹב הַדָּבָר	1 Kings 2.38 The word is good.
11.	טוֹב יְהוָה	Psalm 34.8 Yahweh is good.
12.	אִישׁ טוֹב	2 Sam. 18.27 a good man
13.	אֶרֶץ טוֹבָה	Exodus 3.8 a good land

Part 2: Translate the following English into Hebrew:

1.   Good men   אֲנָשִׁים טוֹבִים
2.   The fathers are good.   טוֹבִים הָאָבוֹת
3.   The day is good.   טוֹב הַיּוֹם
4.   The daughter is good.   טוֹבָה הַבַּת

Exercise 3-B

Part 1:

Add the conjunction to the following words and write their translations:

אָדָם	וְאָדָם	and Adam/a human
אֲדָמָה	וַאֲדָמָה	and land/ground/earth
אִישׁ	וְאִישׁ	and a man
אִשָּׁה	וְאִשָּׁה	and a woman
בֵּן	וּבֵן	and a son
בַּת	וּבַת	and a daughter
אֶרֶץ	וְאֶרֶץ	and a land
בַּיִת	וּבַיִת	and a house

Part 2: Translate the following Hebrew into English:

וּמְלָכִים רַבִּים	and many kings	Jer 50.41
וְיוֹם טוֹב	and a good day	Est 8.17
וּמְלָכִים גְּדוֹלִים	and great kings	Jer 25.14

Exercise 3-C

Part 1:

Translate the following sentences from Hebrew into English:

1. וְהַמֶּלֶךְ הַטּוֹב שָׁמַר הַבֵּן וְהַבַּת

2. רַבִּים אֲנָשִׁים וְרָעִים הֹלְכִים אֶל הַבַּיִת

3. וְעַתָּה נָשִׁים טוֹבוֹת הֹלְכוֹת אֶל הָאָרֶץ

4. אֱלֹהִים הַמֶּלֶךְ הַגָּדוֹל

5. מַלְכָּה טוֹבָה הֹלֶכֶת אֶל הָהָר הַגָּדוֹל

6. וְהָאַחִים שֹׁמְרִים הַדָּבָר

7. טוֹבִים הַמְּלָכִים וְגָדוֹל הַבַּיִת

8. הָאֲדָמָה וְהָאָרֶץ שְׁמוּרוֹת

Answers:

1. And the good king is/was keeping/guarding the son and the daughter.
2. Many evil men are going unto the house. (Note: A second attributive adjective [וְרָעִים] is expressed by means of the conjunction)
3. And now, good women are going unto the land.
4. The great king is God. OR God is the great king. (Note: the word order in this verbless clause is ambiguous because it could be construed either as a clause of identification or of specification.
5. A good queen is/was going unto the great mountain.
6. And the brothers are keeping the word.
7. The kings are good and the house is great.
8. The ground/earth and the land/country are being kept. Note: the words 'ground/earth' and 'land/country' sometimes seem to overlap in meaning.

Part 2:

Translate the following sentences from English into Hebrew:

1. The good word is being kept.   הַדָּבָר הַטּוֹב שָׁמוּר

2. The queen is keeping the word.   הַמַּלְכָּה שֹׁמֶרֶת הַדָּבָר

3. The big house is being guarded (kept). הַבַּיִת הַגָּדוֹל שָׁמוּר

4. A good man is keeping the word.   אִישׁ טוֹב שֹׁמֵר הַדָּבָר

5. Now the king is the one keeping the word. עַתָּה הַמֶּלֶךְ הַשֹּׁמֵר הַדָּבָר

CHAPTER 4

Exercise 4-A

Translate the following:

1. הָאָרֶץ שָׁמַרְתְּ:

2. הָאִשָּׁה וְהָאִישׁ שָׁמְרוּ הָאָרֶץ:

3. אִישׁ שָׁמַר הַבַּיִת:

4. הָאָרֶץ שְׁמַרְתֶּם:

5. הָאִשָּׁה שָׁמְרָה הָהָר:

6. הַדָּבָר שָׁמַרְנוּ:

7. הַדָּבָר שָׁמַרְתִּי:

8. הַבֵּן שָׁמַרְתָּ:

Answers:

1. You kept (f sg) the land.
2. The woman and the man/husband kept the land.
3. A man kept the house.
4. You (m.pl.) kept the land.
5. The woman kept the mountain.
6. We kept the word.
7. I kept the word.
8. You (m.sg.) kept the son.

Exercise 4-B

Part 1: Translate the following Hebrew sentences into English.

1. הַמֶּלֶךְ הַטּוֹב שָׁמַר ¹אֶת־הַבֵּן וְאֶת־הַבַּת:

2. וַאֲנָשִׁים רַבִּים הָלְכוּ אֶל הַבָּיִת:

3. וְהַנָּשִׁים הַטּוֹבוֹת הָלְכוּ מִן הָהָר:

4. אֲנִי יָדַעְתִּי אֶת־הַמֶּלֶךְ הַגָּדוֹל:

5. וְרָחֵל אָמְרָה לֵאמֹר מִי עָלָה מִן הַדֶּרֶךְ אֶל הָהָר הַגָּדוֹל:

6. וְאַתָּ אָמַרְתָּ לֵאמֹר עָלָה הָאִישׁ לֵאלֹהִים:

7. וְהַמֶּלֶךְ הַגָּדוֹל זָכַר אֶת־הַבָּנִים וְהַבָּנוֹת:

8. אַתֵּן זְכַרְתֶּן אֶת־הָאָח אֲשֶׁר בַּבָּיִת:

9. וְיַעֲקֹב יָדַע אֶת־הַכֹּהֵן אֲשֶׁר כְּאָח:

10. הָאִשָּׁה יָשְׁבָה בַּבָּיִת הַגָּדוֹל וְהִיא שֹׁמֶרֶת אֶת־הַדָּבָר:

11. אַתְּ אָמַרְתְּ לֵאמֹר מִי עָלָה אֶל הָהָר:

12. וְהַכֹּהֵן הָרָע זָכַר אֶת־הָאִישׁ הַשֹּׁמֵר אֶת־הַדָּבָר:

13. כַּכֹּהֵן זָכַרְתָּ אֶת־הַדָּבָר וְאַתָּה שֹׁמֵר אֶת־הַדָּבָר:

14. אֲנַחְנוּ זֹכְרִים אֶת־כָּל־הַדְּבָרִים אֲשֶׁר אָמַרְתָּ:

15. וְעַתָּה הוּא יֹשֵׁב בַּבָּיִת הַגָּדוֹל:

---

¹ אֶת is the sign of the definite object. It is not translated, but it identifies the following noun as an object of the verb rather than the subject of the verb.

16. וְיַעֲקֹב אָמַר לֵאמֹר שֹׁמְרִים אֲנַחְנוּ אֶת־הַדָּבָר הַטּוֹב:

17. הֵנָּה זֹכְרוֹת אֶת־הַדָּבָר אֲשֶׁר אָמַר יַעֲקֹב בַּדֶּרֶךְ:

18. וְאַתָּה שֹׁמֵר אֶת־הַמֶּלֶךְ:

Answers:

1. The good king kept the son and the daughter.
2. And many men went unto the house.
3. And the good women went from the mountain.
4. I know the great king (The perfect of יָדַע is usually translated present tense).
5. And Rachel said, 'Who went up from the way unto the great mountain?'
6. And you (m.sg.) said, 'The man went up to God'.
7. And the great king remembered the sons and the daughters.
8. You (f.pl.) remembered the brother who (was) in the house.
9. And Jacob knows the priest who (is) like a brother.
10. The woman dwelt in the great house and she was keeping the word.
11. You (f.sg.) said, 'Who went up to the mountain?'
12. And the evil priest remembered the man who was keeping the word.
13. Like the priest, you (m.sg.) remembered the word, and you are keeping the word.
14. We are remembering all the words that you (m.sg.) said.
15. And now, he (is) dwelling in the great house.
16. And Jacob said, 'We are keeping the good word'.
17. They (f.pl.) are remembering the word which Jacob said in the way.
18. And you (m.sg.) are keeping/guarding the king.

Part 2:

Translate the following English sentences into Hebrew.

1. The priest knew the way.
2. And all the priests remembered the good words.
3. The son is remembering the words which the mother said.
4. Who is the man who remembered the king.
5. And the good man went up to the priests who knew the king.

Answers:

1. הַכֹּהֵן יָדַע הַדֶּרֶךְ:

2. וְכָל־הַכֹּהֲנִים זָכְרוּ הַדְּבָרִים הַטּוֹבִים:

3. הַבֵּן זֹכְרִים הַדְּבָרִים אֲשֶׁר אָמְרָה הָאֵם:

4. מִי הָאִישׁ אֲשֶׁר זָכַר הַמֶּלֶךְ:

5. וְהָאִישׁ הַטּוֹב עָלָה לַכֹּהֲנִים אֲשֶׁר יָדְעוּ הַמֶּלֶךְ:

CHAPTER 5

Exercise 5-A

Part 1:

Translate the following Hebrew into English:

וְאֶת־הַיּוֹם הַטּוֹב נִזְכֹּר: 1.

תִּזְכֹּר הָאֵם אֶת־הַבַּת: 2.

אַתֶּן תִּזְכֹּרְנָה אֶת־הַמַּלְכָּה: 3.

וְיַעֲקֹב יִשְׁמֹר אֶת־הַדָּבָר: 4.

תִּזְכְּרוּ אֶת־הָאָרֶץ: 5.

יִזְכְּרוּ אֶת־הַמֶּלֶךְ הַטּוֹב: 6.

וֵאלֹהִים אָמַר אֶזְכֹּר אֶת־הַכֹּהֵן: 7.

Answers:

1. And we shall remember the good day.
2. Let the mother remember the daughter.
3. You (f.pl.) will remember the queen.
4. And Jacob will keep the word.
5. You must/May you remember the land.
6. May they remember the good king.
7. And God said, "I WILL remember the priest."

Part 2:

Translate the following English into Hebrew:

1. May Rachel remember the word.

תִּזְכֹּר רָחֵל אֶת־הַדָּבָר:

2. Rachel will keep the word.

רָחֵל תִּשְׁמֹר אֶת־הַדָּבָר:

3. Let us remember the way.

נִזְכֹּר אֶת־הַדֶּרֶךְ:

Exercise 5-B

Translate the following:

אֲבִי יַעֲקֹב	The father of Jacob	1.
בְּנוֹת רָחֵל	The daughters of Rachel	2.
אִשָּׁה לַמֶּלֶךְ	A wife of the king	3.
נְשֵׁי הַמֶּלֶךְ	The wives of the king	4.

5.	The kings of the earth	מַלְכֵי הָאָרֶץ	
6.	The words of God	דִּבְרֵי אֱלֹהִים	

Exercise 5-C

Translate the following:

1. עִבְרִי עַתָּה בָּאָרֶץ:
2. עֲמֹד בַּדֶּרֶךְ כַּמֶּלֶךְ:
3. כִּתְבוּ דָּבָר טוֹב אֶל־הַכֹּהֵן:
4. זְכֹרְנָה אֶת־רוּחַ יהוה:
5. שִׁמְרִי הַתּוֹרָה מִן־יוֹם לְיוֹם:

Answers:

1. Pass over (f.sg.) now into the land.
2. Stand (m.sg.) in the way like the king.
3. Write (m.pl.) a good word unto the priest.
4. Remember (f.pl.) the Spirit of Yahweh.
5. Keep (f.sg.) the law/instruction from day to day.

Exercise 5-D

Translate the following Hebrew sentences into English.

1. וְלֹא יִשְׁמֹר הַכֹּהֵן הָרָשָׁע אֵת תּוֹרַת אֱלֹהִים:
2. כֹּה אָמַר אֱלֹהִים שִׁמְרִי אֶת־הַמֶּלֶךְ וְאֶת־הַמַּלְכָּה:
3. תִּכְתֹּב הָאִשָּׁה אֶת־דָּבָר רַע אֶל־הָאָח:
4. וְלֹא יִמְלֹךְ הַמֶּלֶךְ עַד יִזְכֹּר אֶת־דִּבְרֵי הַתּוֹרָה:
5. וְאֶת־הָאָרֶץ אֶפְקֹד אָמַר אֱלֹהִים כִּי אַתָּה הֹלֵךְ בְּדֶרֶךְ הַתּוֹרָה:
6. מָה תִּזְכְּרוּ מִן הָרַבִּים הַדְּבָרִים אֲשֶׁר כָּתְבוּ:
7. וּמֹשֶׁה עָמַד בָּהָר הַגָּדוֹל וְלֹא שָׁמְרוּ הָאֲנָשִׁים וְאֶת־דִּבְרֵי־אֱלֹהִים וְאֶת־תּוֹרַת אֱלֹהִים:
8. וְרוּחַ אֱלֹהִים תִּפְקֹד בֶּן־יַעֲקֹב אֲשֶׁר לִפְנֵי הַכֹּהֵן:
9. נִמְלַךְ בְּבֵית־אֱלֹהִים אָמְרוּ מַלְכֵי־הָאָרֶץ:
10. בְּנֵי יַעֲקֹב יָשְׁבוּ בָּאָרֶץ עַד עָלָה הַכֹּהֵן לְהַר אֱלֹהִים:
11. וְעַתָּה מִי יִמְלֹךְ לִפְנֵי־אֱלֹהִים כְּדָוִד:
12. אֶחָד אִישׁ יָדַע כִּי הָאֵם יָלְדָה בֵּן טוֹב:
13. מִי יִמְלֹךְ בָּאָרֶץ הַיּוֹם:

14 כְּתוּבִים דִּבְרֵי־אֱלֹהִים בְּבֵית־אֱלֹהִים:

15. יִכְתֹּב הָאָדָם לַמֶּלֶךְ:

16. וְהָאֲנָשִׁים עָמְדוּ לִפְנֵי־אֱלֹהִים:

17. תִּפְקֹד רוּחַ־אֱלֹהִים אֶת־בֵּית אֱלֹהִים:

18. מָה יִכְתֹּב כִּי יִכְתֹּב לַמֶּלֶךְ:

19. וְלֹא נִפְקֹד אֶת־הַמֶּלֶךְ אֲשֶׁר לֹא יָדַע אֶת־דְּבַר אֱלֹהִים:

20. וְרָחֵל אָמְרָה לֵאמֹר טוֹבִים דִּבְרֵי־אֱלֹהִים:

Answers:

1. And the wicked priest will not keep the law/instruction of God.
2. Thus said/says God, 'Keep/guard (f.sg.) the king and the queen.
3. Let the woman write an evil word unto the brother.
4. And the king will not reign until he remembers the words of the law/instruction.
5. 'And I shall visit the land', said/says God, 'because you (m.sg.) are going in the way of the law/instruction'.
6. What will you (m.pl.) remember from the many words which they wrote?
7. And Moses stood in the great mountain, and the men did not keep the words of God and/or the law/instruction of God.
8. And the Spirit of God will visit (f.sg.) the son of Jacob who (is) before the priest.
9. 'Let us reign in the house of God', said the kings of the earth.
10. The sons of Jacob dwelt in the land until the priest went up to the mountain of God.
11. And now, who will reign before God like David?
12. A certain man knows that the mother bore a good son. (*There is no specific Hebrew word that means 'certain'; instead the word* אֶחָד *is used.*)
13. Who will reign in the land today?
14. The words of God are written in the house of God.
15. Let the man write to the king.
16. And the men stood before God.
17. Let the Spirit of God visit the house of God.
18. What will he write when he writes to the king?
19. And we shall not visit the king who does not know the word of God.
20. And Rachel said, 'The words of God are good'.

CHAPTER 6

Exercise 6-A

Translate the following from Hebrew to English:

נִזְכְּרָה אֶת־הַתּוֹרָה:	Let us remember the law.	1.
וְלֹא תִפְקֹד הַבַּיִת הָרַע:	And you shall not visit the evil house.	2.
וְאַל תִּזְכְּרוּ אֶת־דֶּרֶךְ־הָרָשָׁע:	And do not remember the way of the wicked.	3.
אֶעְבְּרָה הַהַר הַגָּדוֹל:	I WILL pass over the great mountain. Or, Let me pass over the great mountain.	4.

Exercise 6-B

Translate the following sentences.

1. אַנְשֵׁי־יְרוּשָׁלַם יָצְאוּ מִן הַמֶּלֶךְ וְאֵלֶיךָ הָלְכוּ:
2. וַאֲחִי־הַכֹּהֵן יָצָא עִם בְּנוֹ לַנָּהָר:
3. וְהִנֵּה אָכְלוּ אֶת־הַלֶּחֶם הֶחָדָשׁ:
4. וְלֹא עָמַד יִשְׂרָאֵל וּבְנוֹתָיו לִפְנֵי הַמֶּלֶךְ:
5. אִכְלוּ הַלֶּחֶם אֲשֶׁר לְקַחְתֶּם לָכֶם:
6. כֹּה אָמַר יהוה אֶפְקְדָה אֶתְכֶם:
7. לִקְחוּ דְּבַר־יהוה אֲשֶׁר לֶחֶם־הַחַיִּים:
8. מִי הָלַךְ בַּהֵיכָל הַגָּדוֹל אֲשֶׁר בִּירוּשָׁלַם:
9. כְּתֹב אֶל אָבִיךָ לֵאמֹר יֹשֵׁב אֲדֹנִי עַל כִּסְאוֹ:
10. וּמֹשֶׁה עָלָה לָהָר לֵאמֹר יִמְלֹךְ אֱלֹהִים עַל כָּל־הָאָרֶץ:

Answers:
1. The men of Jerusalem went out from the king and they went to you.
2. And the brother of the priest went out with his son to the river.
3. And behold, eat (ye) the new bread.
4. And Israel and his daughters did not stand before the king. (*Note: In Hebrew a singular verb can be used with a compound subject.*)
5. Eat (ye) the bread which you took for yourselves.
6. Thus said Yahweh, I WILL visit you.
7. Take (ye) the word of Yahweh which [is] the bread of life.
8. Who went in the great temple which [is] in Jerusalem
9. Write unto your father saying, 'The Lord is sitting upon his throne.'
10. And Moses went up to the mountain saying, 'Let God/May God reign over all the land'.

26

Exercise 6-C

Translate the following:

1. יָלֹד יָלְדָה רוּחַ־אֱלֹהִים הַתּוֹרָה:
2. עָבֹר עָבְרוּ הַנָּהָר אֵלֶיךָ:
3. וְאַתָּ עָמַדְתָּ עָמֹד לִפְנֵי הַכִּסֵּא:
4. וְהִנֵּה אָכַלְתִּי אָכֹל לֶחֶם־הַחַי:
5. כָּתֹב יִכְתְּבוּ אֵלֵינוּ בַּהֵיכָל:
6. מָלֹךְ יִמְלֹךְ עַל הַכִּסֵּא הֶחָדָשׁ:

Answers:

1. The Spirit of God surely birthed/brought forth the law.
2. They surely passed over the river unto you.
3. And you stood continually before the throne.
4. And behold, I ate continually the bread of life.
5. They will surely write unto us in the temple.
6. He will surely reign upon the new throne.

Exercise 6-D

Translate the following:

1. וּמֹשֶׁה יָצָא לִפְקֹד עִם הַכֹּהֵן הַטּוֹב:
2. וּמֹשֶׁה אָמַר לַעֲמֹד בְּדֶרֶךְ יהוה:
3. אֶזְכֹּר כְּתָבְכֶם לִי אֶת־דְּבַר־יהוה:
4. וּמֹשֶׁה יָדַע כִּי־טוֹב מָלְכוֹ עַל הָאָרֶץ:

Answers:

1. And Moses went out to visit with the good priest.
2. And Moses said to stand in the way of Yahweh.
3. I WILL remember your writing to me the word of Yahweh. Or,
   May I remember your writing to me the word of Yahweh.
4. And Moses knew/knows that his reigning over the land is good.

CHAPTER 7

Exercise 7-A

Translate the following:

וַאֲנַחְנוּ אָכַלְנוּ אֶת־לַחְמֵנוּ וַנִּזְכֹּר דְּבַר־יהוה׃   1.

We ate our bread and we remembered the word of Yahweh.

וְיִצְחָק יָצָא מִן־הַהֵיכָל וַיִּזְכֹּר אֶת־הַדֶּרֶךְ הַטּוֹב׃   2.

Isaac went out from the temple and he remembered the good way.

Exercise 7-B

Find the following Hebrew words in your Hebrew lexicon. List the page number and the main definitions. *Note: the page number will depend upon which lexicon the student uses. For purposes of this answer key, we will use Holladay's* Lexicon of Biblical Hebrew and Aramaic *(1988 edn).*

	Page	Definition
נֹכַח	238	opposite, in front of
עֹלָה	273	burnt offering
חָשַׁךְ	119	become dark
בָּנָה	42	*Qal*-build; *Nifal*-be built, have a child
פְּרִי	297	fruit, result, offspring
שָׁלַח	371	*Qal*-let go, stretch out, send; *Pual*-be sent; *Hifil*-let loose

Exercise 7-C

Translate the following sentences.

יהוה יִדְרֹשׁ אֶת יַעֲקֹב וְנָתַן אֵלָיו לֵב חָדָשׁ׃   1.

פָּקֹד אֶפְקֹד אֹתָךְ אָמַר אֱלֹהִים וְיָלַדְתְּ בֵּן׃   2.

וּבְרֵאשִׁית יָשַׁב אַבְרָהָם בְּאֶרֶץ־כְּנַעַן וַיִּכְרֹת בְּרִית עִם יֹשְׁבֵי־הָאָרֶץ׃   3.

וּמֹשֶׁה יָרַד מִן הַהַר וַיִּדְרֹשׁ אַחֲרֵי אֶחָיו׃   4.

וְהָאֲנָשִׁים הָרָעִים נָשְׂאוּ יְדֵיהֶם עַל מֹשֶׁה וַיִּזְכֹּר מֹשֶׁה דְּבַר־יהוה׃   5.

יֵשׁ דֶּרֶךְ־חַי אִם תִּדְרְשׁוּ אֹתוֹ׃   6.

תִּדְרֹשׁ נַפְשְׁךָ אֶת־יהוה׃   7.

וְיַעֲקֹב נָשָׂא אֶת־לְבָבוֹ אֶל־יהוה וַיִּשְׁמֹר דְּבָרָיו׃   8.

9. חַיָּה רָעָה אֲכָלָתְהוּ: (Gen. 37.33)

10. וְשָׁאוּל לֹא אָכַל לֶחֶם כָּל־הַיּוֹם: (1 Sam. 28.20)

11. וַיִּכְתֹּב מֹשֶׁה אֵת כָּל־דִּבְרֵי יְהוָה: (Exod. 24.4)

12. וַיִּמְלֹךְ דָּוִד עַל־כָּל־יִשְׂרָאֵל: (2 Sam. 8.15)

13. וַיִּמְלֹךְ שְׁלֹמֹה בִירוּשָׁלַם עַל־כָּל־יִשְׂרָאֵל: (2 Chron. 9.30)

14. וַיִּזְכֹּר אֱלֹהִים אֶת־נֹחַ וְאֵת כָּל־הַחַיָּה: (Gen. 8.1)

15. וַיִּזְכֹּר אֱלֹהִים אֶת־בְּרִיתוֹ: (Exod. 2.24)

16. וְלֹא זָכְרוּ בְּנֵי יִשְׂרָאֵל אֶת־יְהוָה אֱלֹהֵיהֶם: (Judg. 8.34)

17. וַיהוָה פָּקַד אֶת־שָׂרָה כַּאֲשֶׁר אָמָר: (Gen. 21.1)

18. וַיִּפְקֹד שִׁמְשׁוֹן אֶת־אִשְׁתּוֹ: (Judg. 15.1)

19. וּמִן־הָאָרֶץ יָצָא אַשּׁוּר: (Gen. 10.11)

20. וְהִיא הָלְכָה לִדְרֹשׁ אֶת־יְהוָה: (Gen. 25.22)

Answers:

1. Yahweh will seek Jacob and he will give unto him a new heart.
2. 'I will surely visit you', said/says God, 'and you will bear a son'.
3. And in the beginning, Abraham dwelled in the land of Canaan, and he made (cut) a covenant with the inhabitants of the land.
4. And Moses went down from the mountain, and he sought after his brothers.
5. And the evil men lifted their hands against Moses, and Moses remembered the word of Yahweh.
6. There is a way of life if you will seek it.
7. May/let your soul seek Yahweh.
8. And Jacob lifted his heart unto Yahweh, and he kept his words.
9. An evil beast ate him.
10. And Saul did not eat bread all the day.
11. And Moses wrote all the words of Yahweh.
12. And David reigned over all Israel.
13. And Solomon reigned in Jerusalem over all Israel.
14. And God remembered Noah and every living thing.
15. And God remembered his covenant.
16. And the sons of Israel did not remember Yahweh their God.
17. And Yahweh visited Sarah as he had said.
18. And Samson visited his wife.
19. And Asshur went out from the land.
20. And she went to seek/inquire of Yahweh.

CHAPTER 8

Exercise 8-A

Translate the following: (You may need to consult the biblical context).

1. וְרַבִּים דְּבָרִים נִזְכְּרוּ הַיּוֹם:
2. וְנַפְשׁוֹ נִלְקְחָה אֶל אֱלֹהִים:
3. וּבַת־הַמֶּלֶךְ נִשְׁלְחָה אֶל הַהֵיכָל:
4. תּוֹרַת אֱלֹהִים לֹא נִשְׁמְרָה בִּימֵי־אֲבוֹתֵיכֶם:
5. וְנִזְכַּרְתֶּם לִפְנֵי יְהוָה אֱלֹהֵיכֶם: (Num. 10.9)
6. וַאֲרוֹן אֱלֹהִים נִלְקָח: (1 Sam. 4.11)
7. נִלְכְּדָה הָעִיר: (1 Kgs 16.18)

Answers:

1. And many words were remembered today.
2. And his soul was taken unto God.
3. And the daughter of the king was sent unto the temple.
4. The law/instruction of God was not kept in the days of your fathers.
5. And you will be remembered/mentioned before Yahweh your God.
6. And the ark of God was taken.
7. The city was captured.

Exercise 8-B

Translate the following:

1. אַתֵּן תִּזָּכַרְנָה בְּבֵית הַמֶּלֶךְ:
2. אֲנַחְנוּ נִנָּתֵן אֶת־חַיִּים מִן־רוּחַ־יהוה:
3. וְהִנֵּה רָחֵל תִּפָּקֵד בַּדֶּרֶךְ בְּאִישׁ מִן־אֱלֹהִים:
4. וּמֶלֶךְ רָע לֹא־יִזָּכֵר:
5. וּבְכֹל אֲשֶׁר־אָמַרְתִּי אֲלֵיכֶם תִּשָּׁמֵרוּ: (Exod. 23.13)
6. מִן־כֹּל אֲשֶׁר־אָמַרְתִּי אֶל־הָאִשָּׁה תִּשָּׁמֵר: (Judg. 13.13)
7. וְלֹא־יִכָּרֵת לְךָ אִישׁ מִן־לְפָנַי יֹשֵׁב עַל־כִּסֵּא יִשְׂרָאֵל: (1 Kgs 8.25)
8. וּרְשָׁעִים מִן־הָאָרֶץ יִכָּרֵתוּ: (Prov. 2.22)
9. וְאִישׁ עִם־אִשָּׁה יִלָּכֵדוּ: (Jer. 6.11)

Answers:

1. You will be remembered in the house of the king.
2. We will be given life from the Spirit of Yahweh.
3. And behold, Rachel will be visited in the way by a man from God.

---

[2] Idiom meaning *today*.

4. And an evil king will not be remembered.
5. And in all which I said unto you, you shall take heed (be guarded).
6. From all which I said unto the woman, let her take heed/beware.
7. And there shall not be cut off for you a man from before me, sitting on the throne of Israel.
8. And the wicked will be cut off from the land.
9. And a man with (his) wife will be captured/seized.

Exercise 8-C

Translate the following sentences:

1. הִשָּׁמֶר לְךָ וּשְׁמֹר נַפְשְׁךָ: (Deut. 4.9)

2. הִשָּׁמְרוּ לָכֶם וְזִכְרוּ אֶת־בְּרִית יְהוָה אֱלֹהֵיכֶם אֲשֶׁר כָּרַת עִמָּכֶם: (Deut. 4.23)

3. הִנָּשֵׂא שֹׁפֵט הָאָרֶץ: (Ps. 94.2)

Answers:

1. Take heed to yourself, and guard your soul.
2. Take heed to yourselves and remember (imperative)the covenant of Yahweh your God who made (cut) it with you.
3. Be lifted up, Judge of the earth.

Exercise 8-D

Part 1:

Translate the following:

1. וְלֹא־יִקָּרֵא עוֹד אֶת־שִׁמְךָ אַבְרָם וְהָיָה שִׁמְךָ אַבְרָהָם: (Gen. 17.5)

2. וַיֹּאמֶר אֱלֹהִים אֶל־אַבְרָהָם בְּיִצְחָק יִקָּרֵא לְךָ זָרַע: (Gen. 21.12)

3. וַיֹּאמֶר־לוֹ אֱלֹהִים שִׁמְךָ יַעֲקֹב לֹא־יִקָּרֵא שִׁמְךָ עוֹד יַעֲקֹב כִּי־אִם וְהָיָה שִׁמְךָ יִשְׂרָאֵל: (Gen. 35.10)

4. וַיֹּאמֶר הִנֵּה אָנֹכִי כֹּרֵת בְּרִית: (Exod. 34.10)

5. וַיִּלָּכֵד יוֹנָתָן וְשָׁאוּל וְהָעָם יָצָאוּ: (1 Sam. 14.41)

6. וַיִּקְרָא לָהּ יַד אַבְשָׁלוֹם עַד הַיּוֹם הַזֶּה: (2 Sam. 18.18)

7. נִשְׁבְּרוּ לִפְנֵי־יְהוָה: (2 Chron. 14.12, Eng. is v. 13)

8. וּמִבְּנֵי הַכֹּהֲנִים בְּנֵי חֲבַיָּה בְּנֵי הַקּוֹץ בְּנֵי בַרְזִלַּי אֲשֶׁר לָקַח מִן־בְּנוֹת בַּרְזִלַּי הַגִּלְעָדִי אִשָּׁה וַיִּקָּרֵא עַל־שְׁמָם: (Ezra 2.61)

9. יִקָּרֵא שִׁמְךָ עָלֵינוּ: (Isa. 4.1)

10. אֱלֹהֵי כָל־הָאָרֶץ יִקָּרֵא: (Isa. 54.5)

11.   וְאַתֶּם כֹּהֲנֵי יְהוָה תִּקָּרֵאוּ: (Isa. 61.6)

12.   וַיִּקְרָא שְׁמָהּ בָּמָה עַד הַיּוֹם הַזֶּה: (Ezek. 20.29)

Answers:

1.   And your name shall not again be called 'Abram', but your name shall be 'Abraham'.
2.   And God said unto Abraham, 'In Isaac your seed shall be called'.
3.   And God said to him, 'Your name is "Jacob", your name shall not again be called 'Jacob,' but rather your name shall be "Israel"'.
4.   And he said, 'Behold, I am making (cutting) a covenant'.
5.   And Jonathan and Saul were captured, but the people escaped (went out). (*Note: Compound subjects often take a singular verb.*)
6.   And it is called 'The Hand of Absalom' until this day.
7.   They were broken before Yahweh.
8.   And from the sons of the priests, the sons of Chabaiyah, the sons of Haqqotz, and the sons of Barzillai (who had taken a wife from the daughters of Barzillai the Gileadite, and was called by their name).
9.   Let your name be called upon us. (That is, Let us be named after you.)
10. He shall be called the God of all the earth/land.
11. And you, you shall be called priests of Yahweh.
12. And its name has been called 'Bamah' until this day.

Part 2:

Parse the following words (*qal* and *nifal* stems). You might want to review §7.9.

Hebrew Word	Stem	State	PGN	Pfx	Sfx	Root	Translation
הָלַכְנוּ	Qal	pf	1c pl	NA	NA	הלך	we went
נִשְׁפַּטְתָּ	Nifal	pf	2m s	NA	NA	שׁפט	you were judged
יָרַד	Qal	pf	3m s	NA	NA	ירד	he went down
תִּזָּכְרוּ	Nifal	imf	2m pl	NA	NA	זכר	you will be remembered
יִכָּרֵת	Nifal	imf	3m s	NA	NA	כרת	he/it will be cut (*or* cut off)

CHAPTER 9

Exercise 9-A

Translate the following.

1. הִמְלַכְתָּ אֶת־עַבְדְּךָ אַחַר דָּוִד אָבִי׃

2. הִנֵּה הַנְּבִיאִים הִשְׁמִיעוּ אֶת־הָעָם אֵת קוֹל יהוה׃

3. שְׁמוּאֵל הִכְתִּיב אָבִיו אֵת דְּבַר אֱלֹהִים׃

4. הִפְקִיד אֹתוֹ בְּבֵיתוֹ וְעַל כָּל־אֲשֶׁר יֶשׁ־לוֹ׃ (Gen. 39.5)

Answers:

1. You caused your servant to reign after David my father.
2. Behold, the prophets caused the people to hear the voice of Yahweh.
3. Samuel caused his father to write the word of God.
4. He made him overseer in his house and over all which was his.

Exercise 9-B

Translate the following.

1. הִנֵּה שָׁמַעְתִּי אֶת קוֹלְכֶם כְּכֹל אֲשֶׁר אֲמַרְתֶּם וָאַמְלֵךְ עֲלֵיכֶם מֶלֶךְ׃

2. הַכֹּהֲנִים יַשְׁמִיעוּ אֶתְכֶם אֶת־הַתּוֹרָה מִפִּי־יהוה׃

3. מֹשֶׁה אָמַר אַדְרִישׁ אֶת־נַפְשִׁי אֶת־אֱלֹהִים׃

4. אַזְכִּירָה שִׁמְךָ בְּכָל־דֹּר׃ (Ps. 45.18)

5. וַיַּמְלֵךְ אֶת־שְׁלֹמֹה בְנוֹ עַל־יִשְׂרָאֵל׃ (1Chron. 23.1)

Answers:

1. Behold, I heard your voice according to all that you said and I caused a king to reign over you.
2. The priests will cause you to hear the Torah from the mouth of Yahweh.
3. Moses said, 'Let me cause my soul to seek God'.
4. I WILL bring to memory your name in every generation.
5. And he caused Solomon his son to reign over Israel.

Exercise 9-C

Translate the following.

1. הַזְכִּירִי אֶת־לִבֵּךְ דִּבְרֵי־הַתּוֹרָה:
2. הַעֲבֵר אֶת־הָעָם הַנָּהָר הַזֶּה:
3. הָאֲנָשִׁים מַעֲמִידִים אֶת־הַנָּבִיא הָרַע לִפְנֵי הָעָם:
4. אֲנִי מַזְכִּיר אֶת־בִּתִּי אֶת־קוֹל־יהוה:
5. אֶת־חֲטָאַי אֲנִי מַזְכִּיר הַיּוֹם: (Gen. 41.9)
6. הֲשֹׁפֵט יַשְׁפִּיט אֱלֹהִים אֶת־רוּחוֹ כֹּל בָּשָׂר שָׁם:
7. יַעֲקֹב יָרַד הֵיכָלָה לְהַקְרִיא אֶת־לִבּוֹ אֶל יהוה:

Answers:

1. Cause your heart to remember the words of the Torah.
2. Cause the people to pass over this river.
3. The men are causing the evil prophet to stand before the people.
4. I am causing my daughter to remember the voice of Yahweh.
5. I am recalling/making mention of my sins today.
6. Surely, God will cause his Spirit to judge all flesh there.
7. Jacob went down to the temple to make his heart cry out unto Yahweh.

Exercise 9-D

Parse the following verbs in *hifil* and *hofal*:

Hebrew Word	Stem	State	PGN	Pfx	Sfx	Root	Translation
מַכְתִּיב	H	ptc	ms	NA	NA	כתב	causing to write
יֻשְׁפַּט	Hof	imf	3ms	NA	NA	שׁפט	he will be caused to judge
וַיַּשְׁמֵר	H	imf w	3ms	ו	NA	שׁמר	and he caused to keep
הַמְלִיכוּ	H	imv	2mp	NA	NA	מלך	Cause to reign!
תַּשְׁמִירוּ	H	imf	2mp	NA	NA	שׁמר	you will cause to keep
הָשְׁמְרוּ	Hof	pf	3cp	NA	NA	שׁמר	they were caused to keep

34

Exercise 9-E

Translate the following sentences from the Bible (Use an English translation to help with names and context).

1. וַיֹּאמֶר מֹשֶׁה זֶה הַדָּבָר אֲשֶׁר אָמַר יְהוָה: (Exod. 16.32)

2. וּבְכֹל אֲשֶׁר־אָמַרְתִּי אֲלֵיכֶם תִּשָּׁמֵרוּ וְשֵׁם אֱלֹהִים אֲחֵרִים לֹא תַזְכִּירוּ: (Exod. 23.13)

3. וְיִשְׁמְעוּ הַכְּנַעֲנִי וְכֹל יֹשְׁבֵי הָאָרֶץ וְהִכְרִיתוּ אֶת־שְׁמֵנוּ מִן־הָאָרֶץ: (Josh. 7.9)

4. יַד בְּנֵי־יִשְׂרָאֵל הָיָה עַל יָבִין מֶלֶךְ־כְּנָעַן עַד אֲשֶׁר הִכְרִיתוּ אֵת יָבִין מֶלֶךְ־כְּנָעַן: (Judg. 4.24)

5. וַיֹּאמֶר יְהוָה אֶל־שְׁמוּאֵל שְׁמַע בְּקוֹלָם וְהִמְלַכְתָּ לָהֶם מֶלֶךְ: (1 Sam. 8.22)

6. כָּל־הָעָם הַגִּלְגָּל וַיַּמְלִכוּ שָׁם אֶת־שָׁאוּל לִפְנֵי יְהוָה בַּגִּלְגָּל (1 Sam. 11.15)

7. וַיֹּאמֶר שְׁמוּאֵל אֶל־כָּל־יִשְׂרָאֵל הִנֵּה שָׁמַעְתִּי בְקֹלְכֶם לְכֹל אֲשֶׁר־אֲמַרְתֶּם לִי וָאַמְלִיךְ עֲלֵיכֶם מֶלֶךְ: (1 Sam. 12.1)

8. וְלֹא־תַכְרִת אֶת־חַסְדְּךָ מֵעִם בֵּיתִי עַד־עוֹלָם (1 Sam. 20.15)

9. הִנֵּה אַתָּה יָדַעְתָּ אֵת אֲשֶׁר־עָשָׂה שָׁאוּל: (1 Sam. 28.9)

10. אֲדֹנֵינוּ הַמֶּלֶךְ־דָּוִד הִמְלִיךְ אֶת־שְׁלֹמֹה: (1 Kgs 1.43)

11. וְעַתָּה יְהוָה אֱלֹהָי אַתָּה הִמְלַכְתָּ אֶת־עַבְדְּךָ תַּחַת דָּוִד אָבִי: (1 Kgs 3.7)

12. וְהִכְרַתִּי אֶת־יִשְׂרָאֵל מֵעַל פְּנֵי הָאֲדָמָה: (1 Kgs 9.7)

13. וַיַּמְלִיכוּ אֹתוֹ תַּחַת אָבִיו אֲמַצְיָהוּ: (2 Kgs 14.21)

14. וַיַּמְלִיכוּ עַם־הָאָרֶץ אֶת־יֹאשִׁיָּהוּ בְנוֹ תַּחְתָּיו: (2 Kgs 21.24)

15. חַסְדֵי יְהוָה אַזְכִּיר: (Isa. 63.7)

16. וְהִכְרַתִּי יוֹשֵׁב מֵאַשְׁדּוֹד: (Amos 1.8)

17. וְהָיָה בַיּוֹם־הַהוּא נְאֻם־יְהוָה וְהִכְרַתִּי סוּסֶיךָ מִקִּרְבֶּךָ: (Mic. 5.9; Eng. is v. 10)

18. וְהִכְרַתִּי עָרֵי אַרְצֶךָ: (Mic. 5.10; Eng. is v. 11)

19. וְהִכְרַתִּי אֶת־הָאָדָם מֵעַל פְּנֵי הָאֲדָמָה נְאֻם־יְהוָה: (Zeph. 1.3)

20. וְהָיָה בַיּוֹם הַהוּא נְאֻם יְהוָה צְבָאוֹת אַכְרִית אֶת־שְׁמוֹת

הָעֲצַבִּים מִן־הָאָרֶץ וְלֹא יִזָּכְרוּ עוֹד: (Zech. 13.2)

21. מֶלֶךְ־מִצְרַיִם אֶת־אֶלְיָקִים אָחִיו עַל־יְהוּדָה וִירוּשָׁלִָם: (2 Chron. 36.4)
וַיַּמְלֵךְ

Answers:

1. And Moses said, 'This is the word that Yahweh said'.
2. And in all which I said unto you, beware, and you shall not mention (bring to remembrance) the name of other gods.
3. And may the Canaanites hear and all the inhabitants of the land, and they will cut off our name from the earth.
4. The hand of the sons of Israel was against Jabin, king of Canaan, until they cut off Jabin, king of Canaan.
5. And Yahweh said unto Samuel, 'Obey (hear) their voice, and cause a king to reign for them'.
6. All the people went to Gilgal and they caused Saul to reign there before Yahweh in Gilgal.
7. And Samuel said unto all Israel, 'Behold, I have obeyed (heard) your voice in regard to all which you said to me'. And I caused a king to reign over you.
8. And you shall not cut off your lovingkindness from my house forever.
9. Behold, you know what Saul did.
10. Our lord, king David, enthroned Solomon.
11. Now Yahweh my God, you have enthroned your servant instead of David my father.
12. And I will cut off Israel from the face of the land.
13. And they enthroned him instead of his father Amaziah.
14. And the people of the land enthroned Josiah his son instead of him.
15. The mercies of Yahweh I will mention (cause to remember).
16. And I will cut off inhabitants from Ashdod.
17. 'And it shall be in that day', saith Yahweh, 'I will cut off your horses from among you'.
18. And I will cut off the cities of your land.
19. 'And I will cut off humanity from the face of the earth', saith Yahweh.
20. 'And it shall be in that day,' saith Yahweh of hosts, 'I will cut off the names of the idols from the land and they will not be remembered again',
21. And the king of Egypt enthroned Eliakim his brother over Judah and Jerusalem.

CHAPTER 10

Exercise 10-A

Translate the following excerpts and paraphrases from Scripture:

Gen. 6.22 כֵּן עָשָׂה נֹחַ כְּכֹל אֲשֶׁר צִוָּה אֹתוֹ אֱלֹהִים כֵּן עָשָׂה:

36

אַבְרָם הָלַךְ כַּאֲשֶׁר דִּבֶּר אֵלָיו יְהוָה: Gen. 12.4

וַיהוה עָשָׂה לְשָׂרָה כַּאֲשֶׁר דִּבֵּר: וַיהוה פָּקַד אֶת־שָׂרָה Gen. 21.1

כַּאֲשֶׁר אָמַר

אֱלֹהִים עָלָה מֵעָלָיו בַּמָּקוֹם אֲשֶׁר־דִּבֶּר אִתּוֹ: Gen. 35.13

וַיְהִי כִּי שָׁמַע אֲדֹנָיו אֶת־דִּבְרֵי אִשְׁתּוֹ אֲשֶׁר דִּבְּרָה Gen. 39.19

אֵלָיו לֵאמֹר כַּדְּבָרִים הָאֵלֶּה עָשָׂה לִי עַבְדֶּךָ:

הוּא הַדָּבָר אֲשֶׁר דִּבַּרְתִּי אֶל־פַּרְעֹה: Gen. 41.28

Answers:

Gen. 6.22   Thus Noah did according to all which God commanded him; thus he did.

Gen. 12.4   Abram walked according to what Yahweh spoke unto him.

Gen. 21.1   So Yahweh visited Sarah according to what he had said; and Yahweh did for Sarah according to what he had spoken.

Gen. 35.13   God went up from him in the place where he had spoken with him.

Gen. 39.19   And it was that his lord heard the words of his wife which she spoke unto him *saying*, "According to these words your servant did to me."

Gen. 41.28   It/that is the word which I spoke unto Pharoah.

Exercise 10-B

Translate the following:

וַיֹּאמְרוּ אֵלָיו לָמָּה יְדַבֵּר אֲדֹנִי כַּדְּבָרִים הָאֵלֶּה: Gen. 44.7

וְאַהֲרֹן אָחִיךָ יְדַבֵּר אֶל־פַּרְעֹה וְשִׁלַּח Exod. 7.2

אֶת־בְּנֵי־יִשְׂרָאֵל מֵאַרְצוֹ:

אֵלֶּה הַדְּבָרִים אֲשֶׁר תְּדַבֵּר אֶל־בְּנֵי יִשְׂרָאֵל: Exod. 19.6

Answers:

Gen. 44.7   And they said unto him, "Why will/would my lord speak according to these words?" (= such words as these)

Exo. 7.2   Aaron your brother will speak unto Pharoah, and he will send forth the sons of Israel from his land.

Exod. 19.6   These are the words which you shall speak unto the sons of Israel

Exercise 10-C

Translate the following:

מַה־תְּבַקֵּשׁ: ...   Gen. 37.15

וַיֹּאמֶר אֶת־אַחַי אָנֹכִי מְבַקֵּשׁ:   Gen. 37.16

וַיִּשְׁמַע פַּרְעֹה אֶת־הַדָּבָר הַזֶּה וַיְבַקֵּשׁ אֶת־מֹשֶׁה: Exod. 2.15

Answers:

Gen. 37.15	What do you seek?
Gen. 37.16	And he said, 'My brothers I am seeking'.
Exod. 2.15	And Pharoah heard this word, and he sought Moses.

Exercise 10-D

Parse the following verbs from the *qal*, *nifal*, *hifil*, *hofal*, and *piel* patterns.

Verb	Stem	State	PGN	Pfx	Sfx	Root	Translation
תְּדַבְּרוּ	P	Imf	2mp	NA	NA	דבר	You will speak
הִזְכַּרְתִּי	H	Pf	1cs	NA	NA	זכר	I caused to remember
מְדַבְּרִים	P	Ptc	mp	NA	NA	דבר	speaking
בִּקֵּשׁ	P	Pf	3ms	NA	NA	בקשׁ	he sought
אֶשָּׁפֵט	N	Imf	1cs	NA	NA	שׁפט	I shall be judged
וַיִּשְׁמֹר	Q	Imf w	3ms	ו	NA	שׁמר	And he kept
דַּבְּרִי	P	Imv	2fs	NA	NA	דבר	Speak!
הָשְׁמַרְתֶּם	Ho	Pf	2mp	NA	NA	שׁמר	You were caused to keep.

Exercise 10-E

Translate the following sentences from the Bible (Use an English translation to help with names and context).

וַיְדַבֵּר מֹשֶׁה כֵּן אֶל־בְּנֵי יִשְׂרָאֵל וְלֹא שָׁמְעוּ אֶל־מֹשֶׁה:	Exod. 6.9
וַיְדַבֵּר מֹשֶׁה לִפְנֵי יְהוָה לֵאמֹר הֵן בְּנֵי־יִשְׂרָאֵל לֹא־שָׁמְעוּ אֵלַי:	Exod. 6.12
וַיְהִי בְּיוֹם דִּבֶּר יְהוָה אֶל־מֹשֶׁה בְּאֶרֶץ מִצְרָיִם:	Exod. 6.28
וַיְדַבֵּר יְהוָה אֶל־מֹשֶׁה לֵּאמֹר אֲנִי יְהוָה דַּבֵּר אֶל־פַּרְעֹה מֶלֶךְ מִצְרַיִם אֵת כָּל־אֲשֶׁר אֲנִי דֹּבֵר אֵלֶיךָ:	Exod. 6.29
עוֹד הָעָם מְזַבְּחִים וּמְקַטְּרִים בַּבָּמוֹת:	1 Kgs 22.44 [43]
וַיְזַבֵּחַ וַיְקַטֵּר בַּבָּמוֹת:	2 Kgs 16.4
וַיִּשְׁפְּכוּ דָם־נָקִי דַּם־בְּנֵיהֶם וּבְנוֹתֵיהֶם אֲשֶׁר זִבְּחוּ לַעֲצַבֵּי כְנָעַן:	Ps. 106.38
עַל־רָאשֵׁי הֶהָרִים יְזַבֵּחוּ:	Hos. 4.13
וַיְדַבֵּר אֱלֹהִים אֶל־נֹחַ לֵאמֹר:	Gen. 8.15
וַיֵּלֶךְ אַבְרָם כַּאֲשֶׁר דִּבֶּר אֵלָיו יְהוָה וַיֵּלֶךְ אִתּוֹ לוֹט	Gen. 12.4
וְרִבְקָה אָמְרָה אֶל־יַעֲקֹב בְּנָהּ לֵאמֹר הִנֵּה שָׁמַעְתִּי אֶת־אָבִיךָ מְדַבֵּר אֶל־עֵשָׂו אָחִיךָ	Gen. 27.6
וַיִּשְׁמַע פַּרְעֹה אֶת־הַדָּבָר הַזֶּה וַיְבַקֵּשׁ לַהֲרֹג אֶת־מֹשֶׁה:	Exod. 2.15
בִּקֵּשׁ יְהוָה לוֹ אִישׁ כִּלְבָבוֹ:	1 Sam. 13.14
וְלָקַחְתִּי אֶתְכֶם מִן־הַגּוֹיִם וְקִבַּצְתִּי אֶתְכֶם מִכָּל־הָאֲרָצוֹת:	Ezek. 36.24
וַיְסַפֵּר הָעֶבֶד לְיִצְחָק אֵת כָּל־הַדְּבָרִים אֲשֶׁר עָשָׂה:	Gen. 24.66
וַיְסַפֵּר יַעֲקֹב לְלָבָן אֵת כָּל־הַדְּבָרִים הָאֵלֶּה:	Gen. 29.13
וַיְסַפֵּר מֹשֶׁה לָעָם אֵת כָּל־דִּבְרֵי יְהוָה:	Exod. 24.3
סַפְּרָה־נָּא לִי אֵת כָּל־הַגְּדֹלוֹת אֲשֶׁר־עָשָׂה אֱלִישָׁע:	2 Kgs 8.4
הַשָּׁמַיִם מְסַפְּרִים כְּבוֹד־אֵל:	Ps. 19.2
אֲשֶׁר שָׁמַעְנוּ וַאֲבוֹתֵינוּ סִפְּרוּ־לָנוּ:	Ps. 78.3
לְסַפֵּר בְּצִיּוֹן שֵׁם יְהוָה:	Ps. 102.22
מֹשֶׁה עָשָׂה וְאַהֲרֹן כַּאֲשֶׁר צִוָּה יְהוָה אֹתָם:	Exod. 7.6
זֶה הַדָּבָר אֲשֶׁר צִוָּה יְהוָה:	Exod. 16.16

Answers:

Exod. 6.9	And Moses said thus unto the sons of Israel, but they did not listen unto Moses.
Exod. 6.12	And Moses spoke before Yahweh saying, "Behold, the Sons of Israel did not listen to me."
Exod. 6.28	And it was in the day Yahweh spoke unto Moses in the land of Egypt,
Exod. 6.29	Yahweh spoke unto Moses saying, "I am Yahweh. Speak unto Pharoah, king of Egypt, all which I am speaking unto you."
1 Kgs 22.44 [43]	Yet the people were sacrificing and burning incense in the high places.
2 Kgs 16.4	And he sacrificed and burned incense in the high places.
Ps. 106.38	And they poured out the blood of their sons and their daughters whom they sacrificed to the idols of Canaan.
Hos. 4.13	Upon the tops (heads) of the mountains they will sacrifice.
Gen. 8.15	And God spoke unto Noah saying,
Gen. 12.4	And Abram went as Yahweh had spoken unto him, and Lot went with him.
Gen. 27.6	And Rebekah said unto Jacob her son saying, "Behold, I heard your father speaking to Esau your brother saying, "
Exod. 2.15	And Pharoah heard this word, and he sought to kill Moses.
1 Sam. 13.14	Yahweh sought for himself a man according to his own heart.
Ezek. 36.24	And I will take you from the nations and I will gather you from all the lands.
Gen. 24.66	And the servant recounted to Isaac all the things which he had done.
Gen. 29.13	And Jacob recounted to Laban all these things.
Exod. 24.3	And Moses recounted to the people all the words of Yahweh.
2 Kgs 8.4	Tell me (Recount to me), please, all the great things which Elisha has done.
Ps. 19.2	The heavens are telling (recounting) the glory of God.
Ps. 78.3	What we heard and our fathers have recounted to us.
Ps. 102.22	To tell (recount) in Zion the name of Yahweh.
Exod. 7.6	Moses and Aaron did as Yahweh had commanded them.
Exod. 16.16	This is the word which Yahweh commanded.

40

CHAPTER 11

Exercise 11-A

Translate the following:

שְׁלֹמֹה הִתְהַלֵּךְ אַחַר דָּוִד אָבִיו: .1

אָדָם הִתְהַלֵּךְ עִם אֱלֹהִים: .2

הִנֵּה לֹא הִתְהַלְּכוּ הָעָם כְּקוֹל נְבִיאֵי־יהוה: .3

Answers:

1. Solomon walked after David his father.
2. Adam walked with God.
3. Behold, the people did not walk according to the voice of the prophets of Yahweh.

Exercise 11-B

Translate the following:

עַתָּה שָׁאוּל יִתְנַשֵּׂא עַל שְׁמוּאֵל וְעַל אֱלֹהִים: .1

הַכֹּהֵן מִתְנַשֵּׂא עַל אֶת־תּוֹרַת־יהוה: .2

מֹשֶׁה דִּבֶּר לֵאמֹר יִתְנַשֵּׂא אֱלֹהִים: .3

Answers:

1. Now Saul will lift up himself over/against Samuel and over/against God.
2. The priest is/was lifting up himself over/against the law/instruction of Yahweh.
3. Moses spoke *saying*, "May God lift up himself."

Exercise 11-C

Translate these verses with *pual* verbs.

שָׁמָּה קֻבַּר אַבְרָהָם וְשָׂרָה אִשְׁתּוֹ: Gen. 25.10

וְהָאֲנָשִׁים שֻׁלְּחוּ: Gen. 44.3

כִּי גָדוֹל יהוה וּמְהֻלָּל מְאֹד: 1 Chr. 16.25

וַיְבֻקַּשׁ הַדָּבָר וַיִּמָּצֵא: Est. 2.23

מְהֻלָּל שֵׁם יהוה: Psa. 113.3

Answers:

Gen. 25.10	There Abraham was buried and Sarah his wife.	
Gen. 44.3	And the men were sent out.	
1 Chr. 16.25	Because great is Yahweh and praised exceedingly.	
Esther 2.23	And the thing/matter was sought and it was found.	
Ps. 113.3	Praised is the name of Yahweh	

Exercise 11-D

Part 1:

Parse the following verbs from the *qal*, *nifal*, *hifil*, *hofal*, *piel*, *pual*, and *hitpael* patterns.

Verb	Stem	State	PGN	Root	Translation
תִּשְׁמְרוּ	Q	imf	2m pl	שׁמר	you shall keep
אַקְטִיל	H	imf	1c s	קטל	I will cause to kill
קֻטְּלָה	Pu	pf	3f s	קטל	she was killed
קַטְּלוּ	P	imv	2m pl	קטל	Kill!
הִתְקַטַּלְנוּ	Ht	pf	1c pl	קטל	we killed ourselves
מְקֻטָּל	Pu	ptc	m s	קטל	being killed
יִתְקַטְּלוּ	Ht	imf	3m pl	קטל	they will kill themselves
שָׁמוּר	Q	p ptc	m s	שׁמר	being kept
מִתְקַטֵּל	Ht	ptc	m s	קטל	killing oneself

Part 2:

Translate the following excerpts from Scripture.

וַיִּשְׁמְעוּ אֶת־קוֹל יְהוָה אֱלֹהִים מִתְהַלֵּךְ בַּגָּן׃   Gen. 3.8

וַיִּתְהַלֵּךְ חֲנוֹךְ אֶת־הָאֱלֹהִים וְאֵינֶנּוּ כִּי־לָקַח אֹתוֹ אֱלֹהִים׃   Gen. 5.24

אֶת־הָאֱלֹהִים הִתְהַלֶּךְ־נֹחַ׃   Gen. 6.9

וַיִּתְפַּלֵּל אַבְרָהָם אֶל־הָאֱלֹהִים׃   Gen. 20.17

וְהִתְבָּרֲכוּ בְזַרְעֲךָ כֹּל גּוֹיֵי הָאָרֶץ׃   Gen. 26.4

וַיֹּאמֶר מֹשֶׁה זֶה הַדָּבָר אֲשֶׁר אָמַר יְהוָה׃   Exod. 16.32

וַיֹּאמְרוּ אֵלֶּה אֱלֹהֶיךָ יִשְׂרָאֵל׃   Exod. 32.4

כִּי אֲנִי יְהוָה אֱלֹהֵיכֶם וְהִתְקַדִּשְׁתֶּם׃   Lev. 11.44

וַיִּתְפַּלֵּל מֹשֶׁה אֶל־יְהוָה:	Num. 11.2
וָאֶתְפַּלֵּל אֶל־יְהוָה:	Deut 9.26
וַיִּשְׁמְעוּ פְלִשְׁתִּים כִּי־הִתְקַבְּצוּ בְנֵי־יִשְׂרָאֵל הַמִּצְפָּתָה:	1 Sam. 7.7
וַיִּתְקַבְּצוּ כֹּל זִקְנֵי יִשְׂרָאֵל אֶל־שְׁמוּאֵל הָרָמָתָה:	1 Sam. 8.4
וַיִּתְפַּלֵּל שְׁמוּאֵל אֶל־יְהוָה:	1 Sam. 8.6
וְעַתָּה הִתְיַצְּבוּ לִפְנֵי יְהוָה:	1 Sam. 10.19
וְעַתָּה הִנֵּה הַמֶּלֶךְ מִתְהַלֵּךְ לִפְנֵיכֶם וַאֲנִי זָקַנְתִּי:	1 Sam. 12.2
וַיֹּאמְרוּ כָל־הָעָם אֶל־שְׁמוּאֵל הִתְפַּלֵּל בְּעַד־עֲבָדֶיךָ אֶל־יְהוָה אֱלֹהֶיךָ:	1 Sam. 12.19
וַיִּתְקַבְּצוּ בְנֵי־בִנְיָמִן אַחֲרֵי אַבְנֵר:	2 Sam. 2.25
וּמֶלֶךְ יִשְׂרָאֵל וִיהוֹשָׁפָט מֶלֶךְ־יְהוּדָה יֹשְׁבִים אִישׁ עַל־כִּסְאוֹ:	1 Kgs 22.10
לוֹא־יִתְנַבֵּא עָלַי טוֹב כִּי אִם־רָע:	1 Kgs 22.18
וַיִּתְפַּלֵּל חִזְקִיָּהוּ לִפְנֵי יְהוָה וַיֹּאמַר יְהוָה אֱלֹהֵי יִשְׂרָאֵל:	2 Kgs 19.15
לָהֶם אַתֶּם רָאשֵׁי הָאָבוֹת לַלְוִיִּם הִתְקַדְּשׁוּ אַתֶּם וַאֲחֵיכֶם: וַיֹּאמֶר	1 Chron. 15.12

Answers:

Gen. 3.8	And they heard the sound of the LORD God walking in the garden.
Gen. 5.24	Enoch walked with God; and he was not, for God took him.
Gen. 6.9	Noah walked with God.
Gen. 20.17	And Abraham prayed to God;
Gen. 26.4	And in your seed all the nations of the earth shall bless themselves.
Exod. 16.32	And Moses said, 'This is the word which Yahweh said.'
Exod. 32.4	And they said, 'These are your Gods, Israel. '
Lev. 11.44	For I am the LORD your God; and you shall consecrate yourselves.
Num. 11.2	And Moses prayed to the LORD
Deut. 9.26	And I prayed to the LORD,
1 Sam. 7.7	And the Philistines heard that the people of Israel had gathered at Mizpah.
1 Sam. 8.4	Then all the elders of Israel gathered together to Samuel at Ramah,
1 Sam. 8.6	And Samuel prayed to the LORD.
1 Sam. 10.19	And now, present yourselves before the LORD
1 Sam. 12.2	And now, behold, the king is walking before you; but I am old
1 Sam. 12.19	And all the people said to Samuel, 'Pray for your servants to the LORD your God. '
2 Sam. 2.25	And the Benjaminites gathered themselves together behind Abner

1 Kgs 22.10	Now the king of Israel and Jehoshaphat the king of Judah were sitting on their thrones,
1 Kgs 22.18	he will not prophesy over me good, but rather evil
2 Kgs 19.15	And Hezekiah prayed before the LORD, and said. 'O LORD the God of Israel.'
1 Chron. 15.12	And he said to them, 'You are the heads of the fathers' houses of the Levites; sanctify yourselves, you and your brothers. '

CHAPTER 12

Exercise 12-A

Translate the following:

וּכְשָׁמְעוֹ אֶת־דִּבְרֵי רִבְקָה אֲחֹתוֹ . . .   Gen. 24.30

וְאַבְרָהָם הֹלֵךְ עִמָּם לְשַׁלְּחָם: Gen. 18.16

נֹחַ עָשָׂה כְּכֹל אֲשֶׁר־צִוָּהוּ יְהוָה: Gen. 7.5

יְהוָה אֱלֹהֵי הַשָּׁמַיִם אֲשֶׁר לְקָחַנִי מִבֵּית אָבִי . . .   Gen. 24.7

יִהְיֶה אֱלֹהִים עִמָּדִי וּשְׁמָרַנִי בַּדֶּרֶךְ הַזֶּה   Gen. 28.20

אֲשֶׁר אָנֹכִי הוֹלֵךְ

Answers:

Gen. 24.30	And when he heard the words of Rebekah his sister . . .
Gen. 18.16	And Abraham was going with them to send them (forth).
Gen. 7.5	Noah did according to all that Yahweh had commanded him.
Gen. 24.7	Yahweh, the God of heaven who took me from the house of my father . . .
Gen. 28.20	Let God be with me and keep me in this way that I am going.

Exercise 12-B—Genesis 1.1-5

> **Q1:** What part of speech is אֵת? *sign of the definite object*

> **Q2:** Is the Hebrew word הַשָּׁמַיִם singular? *no, it is dual*

> **Q3:** Why is there a *dagesh* in the letter *sheen*? *a dagesh follows the definite object*

וְאֵת הָאָֽרֶץ:

> **Q4:** Why does the article take *qamets* instead of *patach*? *because the article precedes the letter alef*

> **Q5:** *Dagesh* follows the article; why is there no *dagesh* in the *alef*? *alef is a guttural, and gutturals do not take the dagesh*

Genesis 1.2

וְהָאָרֶץ

> **Q6:** *Dagesh* follows the article; why is there no *dagesh* in the *alef*? *alef is a guttural*

הָיְתָה *was*

> **Q7:** Why is the verb feminine? *because the subject of the verb is feminine*

תֹהוּ וָבֹהוּ *uninhabited and empty*

> **Q8:** Are these two words nouns or adjectives? *nouns*

> **Q9:** Why is there a *qamets* under the *vav* instead of *sheva*? *because it precedes an accented letter*

וְחֹשֶׁךְ עַל־פְּנֵי

> Is there a verb in this clause? *no* What is the syntactical function of this clause? *This is a verbless clause that functions to provide background. This is a circumstantial clause.*

תְהוֹם *the deep*

וְרוּחַ אֱלֹהִים

> **Q10:** What type of construct–genitive phrase is וְרוּחַ אֱלֹהִים. *Either constituent part, source, or partitive, depending upon the theological interpretation.*

מְרַחֶפֶת *(was) hovering* (PARSE this form) *Piel ptc f s >* רחף

> **Q10:** What does the מְ prefix indicate? *Piel ptc*

> **Q11:** What do the תֶ֫-ֶ vowels and ending indicate? *fem. ptc*

> **Q12:** Does this ptc. function as a substantive, adjective, or verb? *verbal*

> **Q13:** Why is the ptc. feminine? *because the subject is feminine*

עַל־פְּנֵי הַמָּיִם:

> **Q14:** Why is there a *dagesh* in the *mem*? *because it follows the article*

Genesis 1.3

וַיֹּאמֶר אֱלֹהִים   *and God said,*

> **Q15:** What do we call the וַ followed by a *dagesh*? *wayyiqtol*

> **Q16:** What is the י in וַיֹּאמֶר ? *imf preformative*

יְהִי אוֹר   *let there be light*

> **Q17:** What is the י in יְהִי. *imf preformative*

וַיְהִי־אוֹר: *and light was.*

Genesis 1.4

וַיַּרְא *and he saw* (וַ יַ רְא)

> **Q18:** Is this a *wayyiqtol*? *yes*

> **Q19:** What is the י in וַיַּרְא? *imf preformative*

וַיַּבְדֵּל אֱלֹהִים *and God divided* (PARSE וַיַּבְדֵּל) *Hif imf wayyiqtol 3m s >* בדל

> **Q20:** Is this verb a *wayyiqtol*? *yes*

> **Q21:** Why is there a *patach* under the *yod*? *standard vowel of Hifil*

בֵּין הָאוֹר וּבֵין

> **Q22:** Why is there a *qamets* under the ה instead of *patach*? *because the article precedes a guttural alef*

> **Q23:** In וּבֵין, why is the conjunction וּ instead of וְ? *it precedes a labial letter*—מ ב *or* פ

הַחֹשֶׁךְ:   *the darkness*

> **Q24:** The definite article is usually followed by a *dagesh* in the next letter. Why is there no *dagesh* here? *because* ח *is a guttural letter*

Genesis 1.5

(וַ יִ קְרָא) וַיִּקְרָא אֱלֹהִים

> **Q25:** Is וַיִּקְרָא an imperfect? *yes*

> **Q26:** Is it a *wayyiqtol*? *yes*

לָאוֹר יוֹם

> **Q27:** Should לָאוֹר be translated *light* or *the light*? *the light, because the qamets underneath indicates the definite article*

לַחֹשֶׁךְ קָרָא לָיְלָה

Q28: Should לַחֹשֶׁךְ be translated *darkness* or *the darkness*? (§4.4.2) *the darkness, because the patach underneath indicates the definite article*

CHAPTER 13

Exercise 13—Genesis 3.1-6

Genesis 3.1

וְהַנָּחָשׁ

Q1: What is the הַ? *definite article*

Q2: Why is there a *dagesh* in the נ? (§2.3) *a dagesh follows the definite article*

הָיָה עָרוּם

Q3: Parse הָיָה *Q pf 3m s*

מִכֹּל חַיַּת הַשָּׂדֶה

Q4: Is there any difference in meaning between כֹּל and כּוֹל? (§1.8.2) *no, the cholem and the cholem vav have the same meaning and pronunciation*

Q5: The word חַיַּת is from חַיָּה, so why does it end with a ת? *it is in construct*

הַ שָּׂדֶה

Q6: What is the הַ? *definite article*

Q7: Why is there a *dagesh* in the שׂ? (§2.3) *it follows the article*

אֲשֶׁר עָשָׂה יְהוָה אֱלֹהִים

Q8: Parse עָשָׂה *Q pf 3m s*

Q9: Why is עָשָׂה not spelled עָשָׂה? (§12.6.2) *it ends with the ה*

וַיֹּאמֶר אֶל־הָאִשָּׁה

Q10: What part of speech is the י? (§5.1.1) *imf preformative*

Q11: Is וַיֹּאמֶר a *wayyiqtol*? (§13.1.2) *yes*

Q12: Parse וַיֹּאמֶר *Q imf w 3m s*

Q13: What is the הָ in הָאִשָּׁה? *definite article*

Q14: Why is there no *dagesh* in the א? *it is a guttural letter*

אַף כִּי־אָמַר אֱלֹהִים   Williams §383-87

Q15: Parse אָמַר *Q pf 3m s*

לֹא תֹאכְלוּ

Q16: What part of speech is the וּ? (§5.1.1) *imf sufformative, 2m pl*

Q17: Parse תֹאכְלוּ (§13.1.2) *Q imf 2m pl >* אכל

מִכֹּל עֵץ הַגָּן:

Q18: Is עֵץ singular or plural? *singular, used in a collective sense*

הַ גָּן

Q19: What is the הַ? *definite article*

Q20: Why is there a *dagesh* in the גּ? *it follows the article*

Genesis 3.2

וַתֹּאמֶר הָאִשָּׁה

Q21: Why is וַתֹּאמֶר not spelled וַתְּאֹמֶר? (§13.1.2) *it begins with alef*

Q22: What part of speech is the ת in וַתֹּאמֶר? (§5.1.1) *imf preformative*

Q23: Parse וַתֹּאמֶר *Q imf w 3f s >* אמר

מִפְּרִי עֵץ־הַגָּן

Q24: This phrase contains two construct forms. Classify them, §5.3.3. *'Fruit of the tree' is genitive of source, and 'tree of the garden' is partitive or adjectival.*

נֹאכֵל:

Q24: What part of speech is the נֹ? (§5.1.1) *imf preformative*

Q25: Parse נֹאכֵל *Q imf w 1c pl >* אכל

Q26: Why isn't נֹאכֵל spelled נְאֹכֵל? (§13.1.2) *its first root letter is alef*

Genesis 3.3

וּמִפְּרִי הָעֵץ

Q27: What part of speech is the מִ? (§8.4) *preposition*

הָ עֵץ

Q28: What part of speech is the הָ? *definite article*

Q29: Why is the pointing הָ instead of הַ? (§2.3) *it precedes a guttural letter*

אֲשֶׁר בְּתוֹךְ־הַגָּן

Q30: Where is the verb in this clause? *there is no verb; the verb 'to be' is understood*

אָמַר אֱלֹהִים

Q31: Parse אָמַר *Q pf 3m s >* אמר

לֹא תֹאכְלוּ מִמֶּנּוּ

Q32: Analyze and describe מִמֶּנּוּ. (See §8.6.1) *it is the long form of the preposition* מִן *with the pronominal suffix* נוּ *attached*

Q33: Parse תֹּאכְלוּ (§13.1.2) *Q imf 2m pl >* אכל

וְלֹא תִגְּעוּ בּוֹ

Q34: Analyze and describe בּוֹ. (§6.4.3) *preposition* בְּ *with 3m s pronominal suffix attached*

פֶּן־תְּמֻתוּן: Williams §461, §175 *lest you die*

Genesis 3.5

אֲכָל כֶם

Q35: Define/explain כֶם. (§12.3) Williams §109 *pronominal suffix 2m pl*

וְנִפְקְחוּ עֵינֵיכֶם Williams §440

וְ נִ פְקַח וּ

Q36: What part of speech is the וְ? *conjunction*

Q37: What part of speech is the נִ? *Nifal stem indicator*

Q38: Parse וְנִפְקְחוּ *N pf 3c pl >* פקח

Q39: Should וְנִפְקְחוּ be translated as past, present, or future? Why? (§7.3) *future because it is a weqatal (perfect with vav)*

וִהְיִיתֶם כֵּאלהִים

Q40: Parse וִהְיִיתֶם *Q pf 2m pl >* היה

Q41: Should וִהְיִיתֶם be translated as past, present, or future? Why? (§7.3) *future because it is weqatal (perfect with vav)*

יֹדְעֵי טוֹב וָרָע: *knowing good and evil*

Genesis 3.6

וַתֵּרֶא הָאִשָּׁה

Q42: Parse וַתֵּרֶא (§12.6.2) *Q imf w 3f s >* ראה

כִּי טוֹב הָעֵץ לְמַאֲכָל

Q43: Is there a verb in this clause? (§3.2) *no*

וְכִי תַאֲוָה־הוּא לָעֵינַיִם

Find תַאֲוָה in your Hebrew lexicon. *it means 'delight'*

וְנֶחְמָד הָעֵץ לְהַשְׂכִּיל

וְ נֶ חְמָד

Find חָמָד in your lexicon. *it means 'desirable'*

Q44: What is the significance of the וְ? *it functions as a coordinating conjunction, linking the two qualities together—'delight to the eyes and desirable for food'*

Q45: Parse וְנֶחְמָד (see the chart of פ-Guttural verbs) *N ptc m s*

לְ הַ שְׂכִּיל

Q46: What does the infixed י indicate? (§9.2.2) *Hifil*

Q47: What verb form usually has the prefixed preposition? (§6.5.2) *Infinitive construct; however, the participle can also take the preposition.*

וַתִּקַּח מִפִּרְיוֹ

וַ תִּ קַּח   *and she took*

מִ פִּרְי וֹ

Q48: What part of speech is the וֹ? (§6.4.1) *pronominal suffix 3 m s*

וַתֹּאכַל

Q49: Parse וַתֹּאכַל

וַתִּתֵּן גַּם־לְאִישָׁהּ

וַ תִּ תֵּן   *and she gave*

עִמָּהּ וַיֹּאכַל:

עִמָּ הּ

Q50: What part of speech is הּ? (§6.4.3) *pronominal suffix 3 f s*

CHAPTER 14

Exercise 14—Genesis 6.1-8

Genesis 6.1

וַיְהִי כִּי־הֵחֵל הָאָדָם

Q1: PARSE וַיְהִי. *Q imf w 3m s > היה*

The only word in this line that should cause you difficulty is הֵחֵל. It is *hifil* perf. 3ms, from חָלַל, meaning: 1) to defile, 2) to begin. Could this be *double entendre*? How can you determine which meaning applies here? *'Defiled' would require a direct object.* חלל *here means 'begin' because of the infinitive that follows—'began to multiply'*

וּבָנוֹת יֻלְּדוּ לָהֶם:

Q2: What is the וֹת ending? (§2.2.2) *feminine plural ending*

50

Q3: PARSE יֻלְּדוּ *Pual pf 3c pl* > ילד

Genesis 6.2

וַיִּרְאוּ בְנֵי־הָאֱלֹהִים

    Q4: What letter always drops out in the *wayyiqtol*? *final* ה

    Q5: PARSE וַיִּרְאוּ: *Q imf w 3m pl* > ראה

אֶת־בְּנוֹת הָאָדָם כִּי טֹבֹת הֵנָּה

    Q6: Does טֹבֹת have the same meaning as טוֹבוֹת? (§1.8) *yes, cholem and cholem vav are the same*

    Q7: Is there a verb in this clause (כִּי טֹבֹת הֵנָּה)? *no*

מִכֹּל אֲשֶׁר בָּחָרוּ: §26.1.1 #16, Williams §326 & Gesenius §119w, note 2

    Q8: PARSE בָּחֲרוּ *Q pf 3c pl* > בחר

Genesis 6.3

וַיֹּאמֶר יְהוָה

    Q9: PARSE וַיֹּאמֶר: *Q imf w 3m s* > אמר

בְּשַׁגַּם הוּא בָשָׂר

    Q10: Does this clause have a verb? §3.2 *no*

וְהָיוּ יָמָיו מֵאָה וְעֶשְׂרִים שָׁנָה:

    Q11: PARSE וְהָיוּ *Q pf weqatal 3c pl* > היה

    Q12: What happened to the last radical in וְהָיוּ? *final* ה *drops out in some forms*

    Q13: What part of speech is וּ? §6.4.1 *conjunction*

Genesis 6.4

הַנְּפִלִים הָיוּ בָאָרֶץ בַּיָּמִים הָהֵם

    Q14: PARSE הָיוּ *Q pf 3c pl* > היה

    Q15: Does בָאָרֶץ have the definite article? How do you know? (§4.4.2) *yes, the qamets under the* ב *represents the article*

וְגַם אַחֲרֵי־כֵן

אֲשֶׁר יָבֹאוּ בְּנֵי הָאֱלֹהִים אֶל־בְּנוֹת הָאָדָם

    Does יָבֹאוּ refer to an event in the past? *yes* Why is the imperfect used for the past tense? *the imf in past time is used to describe repeated actions*

וְיָלְדוּ לָהֶם   Gesenius §112e

Q16: PARSE וְיָלְדוּ   *Q pf weqatal 3c pl >* ילד

הֵמָּה הַגִּבֹּרִים אֲשֶׁר מֵעוֹלָם אַנְשֵׁי הַשֵּׁם:

אַנְשֵׁי הַשֵּׁם

Q17: Classify the construct–genitive אַנְשֵׁי הַשֵּׁם by referring to §5.3.3. *adjectival*

Genesis 6.5

וַיַּרְא יְהוָה   *and Yahweh saw*

Q18: PARSE וַיַּרְא   *Q imf w 3m s >* ראה

Q19: What happened to the third radical in וַיַּרְא? *the* ה *drops off of the wayyiqtol*

כִּי רַבָּה רָעַת הָאָדָם בָּאָרֶץ   Williams §75, 490, 563, & Gesenius §157b

Q20: Where do we place the unexpressed verb? *after* רַבָּה

Q21: Is רָעַת construct form or absolute form? (§5.6.1) *construct*

Q22: Classify the construct–genitive phrase רָעַת הָאָדָם according to §5.3.3. *characteristic*

וְכָל־יֵצֶר מַחְשְׁבֹת לִבּוֹ רַק רַע כָּל־הַיּוֹם:

Q23: What part of speech is וֹ in לִבּוֹ? (§6.4.3) *pronominal suffix 3m s*

Q24: Classify the construct–genitive phrase מַחְשְׁבֹת לִבּוֹ according to §5.3.3. *genitive of source*

Genesis 6.6

וַיִּנָּחֶם יְהוָה כִּי־עָשָׂה אֶת־הָאָדָם בָּאָרֶץ

The *dagesh* in the נ should alert you that this is not a *qal*. (§8.2.1) *it is a Nifal*

וַיִּתְעַצֵּב אֶל־לִבּוֹ:

Q25: What stem is clearly indicated by the infixed ת ? (§11.2.1) *Hitpael*

Genesis 6.7

וַיֹּאמֶר יְהוָה אֶמְחֶה אֶת־הָאָדָם

Q26: PARSE אֶמְחֶה   *Q imf cohortative 1c s >* מחה

This verb is in first place. What does its position in the clause tell you about its meaning? *the imf in first place is volitive mood (subjunctive)*

אֲשֶׁר־בָּרָאתִי מֵעַל פְּנֵי הָאֲדָמָה

Q27: PARSE בָּרָאתִי   *Q pf 1c s >* ברא

כִּי נִחַמְתִּי כִּי עֲשִׂיתִם:

Q28: PARSE עֲשִׂיתֶם *Q pf 1c s + 3m pl suffix >* עשׂה

Genesis 6.8

וְנֹחַ מָצָא חֵן בְּעֵינֵי יְהוָה:

Q29: Parse מָצָא *Q pf 3m s >* מצא

CHAPTER 15

Exercise 15—Genesis 9.8-17

Genesis 9.8

וַיֹּאמֶר אֱלֹהִים אֶל־נֹחַ וְאֶל־בָּנָיו אִתּוֹ לֵאמֹר:

Q1: What part of speech is the ו on בָּנָיו? (§6.4.1) *pronominal suffix 3m s*

Q2: What part of speech is the וֹ on אִתּוֹ? (§6.4.3) *pronominal suffix 3m s*

Q3: What is the difference between אֹתוֹ and אִתּוֹ? (§6.4.2) *אֹתוֹ is the object pronoun 'him' and* אִתּוֹ *is the preposition 'with' and the pronominal suffix 3m s attached*

Q4: PARSE לֵאמֹר *Q inf cs + prep.* ל *>* אמר

Genesis 9.9

וַאֲנִי הִנְנִי מֵקִים אֶת־בְּרִיתִי אִתְּכֶם

Q5: PARSE מֵקִים *Hif ptc m s >* קום

Q6: What is the difference in meaning between the *qal* and *hifil* of this verb? Consult the lexicon. *the Qal means 'rise' and the Hif means 'raise' or 'establish'*

Q7: Does this ptc. function as a substantive, adj. or verb? *verb*

Genesis 9.10

וְאֵת כָּל־נֶפֶשׁ הַחַיָּה

Q8: The phrase כָּל־נֶפֶשׁ הַחַיָּה is found only four times in Scripture: (Gen. 1.21; 9.10; Lev. 11.10, 46). What does it seem to mean? *every living being*

אֲשֶׁר אִתְּכֶם בָּעוֹף בַּבְּהֵמָה

Q9: Where is the verb in this clause? *There is no verb; the verb 'to be' is implied (§3.2).*

Q10: Why is there a *zaqqef* accent over אִתְּכֶם? *to indicate a pause*

וּבְכָל־חַיַּת הָאָרֶץ אִתְּכֶם

Q11: Why does חַיַּת end with ת instead of ה? *the ה changes to ת in the construct form*

מִכֹּל יֹצְאֵי הַתֵּבָה

Q12: PARSE יֹצְאֵי *Q ptc m pl >* יצא

Q13: Is יֹצְאֵי a substantive, adjective, or verb? *adjective, modifying 'all'*

Q14: Is it past, present, or future time? *past, referring to the departure from the ark, an event in the past*

Genesis 9.11

וַהֲקִמֹתִי אֶת־בְּרִיתִי אִתְּכֶם

Q15: PARSE וַהֲקִמֹתִי *Hif pf 1c s >* קום

Q16: Does וַהֲקִמֹתִי have an imf preformative? *no*

Q17: What is the הֲ? (§15.1.3) *Hif stem indicator*

Q18: In what tense should we translate this verb? *future, because it is weqatal*

וְלֹא־יִכָּרֵת כָּל־בָּשָׂר עוֹד מִמֵּי הַמַּבּוּל

Q19: PARSE יִכָּרֵת *Nif imf 3m s >* כרת

Q20: What stem has *dagesh* in the first root letter of the imf, and *qamets* underneath. *Nifal*

Q21: What voice is יִכָּרֵת: active, passive, reflexive, etc.? *passive*

וְלֹא־יִהְיֶה עוֹד מַבּוּל לְשַׁחֵת הָאָרֶץ׃

Q22: What verb form is most often found with the preposition לְ? *infinitive construct*

Q23: What is the only stem that uses *patach* under the first root letter of the infinitive? (§10.3.5) *Piel*

Q24: Why is there no *dagesh* in the middle radical? (§2.1.2) *it is a guttural letter*

Q25: PARSE לְשַׁחֵת (See §14.2.2) *Piel inf cs >* שחת

Genesis 9.12

וַיֹּאמֶר אֱלֹהִים זֹאת אוֹת־הַבְּרִית

Q26: What part of speech is זֹאת? *demonstrative pronoun*

Q27: How does it function in the clause? *it is the subject in a verbless clause*

אֲשֶׁר־אֲנִי נֹתֵן בֵּינִי וּבֵינֵיכֶם

Q28: PARSE נֹתֵן *Q ptc m s >* נתן

Q29: What kind of action is signified by the ptc.: complete, incomplete, or durative? (§26.1.1 #21) *durative action*

Q30: What is the tense of נֹתֵן? *present tense*

Q31: How many different words have been used to designate the making of this covenant? *this is the third verb:* קום עשׂה *and* נתן

54

Genesis 9.13

אֶת־קַשְׁתִּי נָתַתִּי בֶּעָנָן

Q32: PARSE נָתַתִּי *Q pf 1c s* > נתן

Q33: In what tense should we translate נָתַתִּי? *present tense—performative*

וְהָיְתָה לְאוֹת בְּרִית בֵּינִי וּבֵין הָאָרֶץ:

Q34: PARSE וְהָיְתָה *Q pf 3f s* > היה

Q35: In what tense should we translate וְהָיְתָה? *future, because it is weqatal*

Q36: Explain the presence of ת in this verb. *final ה changes to ת in some forms*

Genesis 9.14

וְהָיָה בְּעַנְנִי עָנָן עַל־הָאָרֶץ

Q37: What verb forms are found with prepositions? *infinitives and participles*

Q38: What is the only stem that uses *patach* under the first root letter of the infinitive? (§10.3.5) *Piel*

Q39: Why is there no *dagesh* in the middle radical? *because it has a sheva under the letter*

Q40: PARSE בְּעַנְנִי *Piel inf cs + 1cs pron. suffix* > ענן

Q41: Is י the subject or object of the infinitive? *subject 'I' (§6.5.2.2).*

וְנִרְאֲתָה הַקֶּשֶׁת בֶּעָנָן:

The ending is pf 3fs, and only one stem of the pf begins with נ. *Nifal*

Q42: PARSE וְנִרְאֲתָה (See §12.6.2) *Nif pf 3f s* > ראה

Q43: How should we translate this verb? (1) *And it shall be seen*, or (2) *And it shall appear*? See (§25.1). This is a *nifal*, middle voice. See also §7.3, §26.1.1 #47. *and it shall appear*

Q44: Why is the *segol* under the preposition in בֶּעָנָן? *because the segol is the pointing for the definite article when it precedes the ayin*

Genesis 9.15

וְזָכַרְתִּי אֶת־בְּרִיתִי

Q45: PARSE וְזָכַרְתִּי *Q pf 1c s* > זכר

Q46: Should this verb be translated in future time? (§7.3, §26.1.1 #47) *Yes, future weqatal.*

וְלֹא־יִהְיֶה עוֹד הַמַּיִם לְמַבּוּל לְשַׁחֵת כָּל־בָּשָׂר:

Q47: PARSE לְשַׁחֵת (See §14.2.2) *Piel Inf cs* > שחת

Genesis 9.16

וְהָיְתָה הַקֶּשֶׁת בֶּעָנָן

> **Q48:** PARSE וְהָיְתָה (See §12.6.2) *Q pf 3f s* > היה

> **Q49:** What is the tense: past, present, or future? *§7.3 future weqatal*

וּרְאִיתִיהָ לִזְכֹּר בְּרִית עוֹלָם

> **Q50:** PARSE וּרְאִיתִיהָ (See §12.6.2) *Q pf 1c s + suffix 3f s* > ראה

> **Q51:** PARSE לִזְכֹּר *Q inf cs* > זכר

Genesis 9.17

וַיֹּאמֶר אֱלֹהִים אֶל־נֹחַ

זֹאת אוֹת־הַבְּרִית אֲשֶׁר הֲקִמֹתִי (§3.2, §7.6)

> **Q52:** PARSE הֲקִמֹתִי (See §15.1.3) *Hif pf 1c s* > קום

> **Q53:** Why does the writer use the perfect? *§26.1.1 #38 and Williams §164*
> *to signify that the action has just now been accomplished*

CHAPTER 16

Exercise 16—Genesis 11.1-9

Genesis 11.1

וַיְהִי כָל־הָאָרֶץ שָׂפָה אֶחָת וּדְבָרִים אֲחָדִים:

> **Q1:** PARSE וַיְהִי (See §12.6.2) *Q imf w 3m s* > היה

> **Q2:** There are two ways to translate וַיְהִי. It can be simply a paragraph marker, or it can function as a real verb. Should we translate as

> 1) *And it came to pass . . .*, or

> 2) *And all the earth was . . . ?* Answer: *2) And all the earth was . . .*

> **Q3:** How do you know which translation is correct? *because there is a subject for the verb here* What is the subject of the verb? *'all the earth'*

> **Q4:** Is אֶחָת an attributive adj. or predicate adjective? Explain. (§3.1.2.1) *attributive, it follow the noun and agrees with it in gender, number, and definiteness*

וּדְבָרִים אֲחָדִים

Genesis 11.2

וַיְהִי בְּנָסְעָם מִקֶּדֶם

> **Q5:** What two verb forms may accept inseparable prepositions? (§6.5.2) *the infinitive and the participle*

Q6: What part of speech is the ם? *pronominal suffix 3m pl*

Q7: Is ם the object or subject of the verbal action? *subject 'they'*

וַיִּמְצְאוּ בִקְעָה בְּאֶרֶץ שִׁנְעָר וַיֵּשְׁבוּ שָׁם:

Q8: PARSE וַיִּמְצְאוּ (See §13.2.2) *Q imf w 3m pl >* מצא

וַיֵּשְׁבוּ *and they dwelled*

Q9: Is the *tsere* under the י the usual vowel for a *qal* imf? (§5.1.1) *no, but this verb begins with yod, which assimilates with the yod preformative and causes the chireq to lengthen to a tsere*

Genesis 11.3

וַיֹּאמְרוּ אִישׁ אֶל־רֵעֵהוּ

Q10: PARSE וַיֹּאמְרוּ *Q imf w 3m pl >* אמר

הָבָה נִלְבְּנָה לְבֵנִים   (Williams §191)

Q11: What is the ה ending on הָבָה? (§6.2) *volitive* ה

Q12: What is the ה ending on נִלְבְּנָה? (§6.1) *volitive* ה

Q13: PARSE נִלְבְּנָה *Q imf coh 1c pl >* לבן

וְנִשְׂרְפָה לִשְׂרֵפָה

Q14: What is the ה ending on וְנִשְׂרְפָה? (§6.1, §26.1.1 #54) *volitive* ה

Q15: PARSE וְנִשְׂרְפָה *Q imf coh 1c pl >* שׂרף

וַתְּהִי לָהֶם הַלְּבֵנָה לְאָבֶן

Q16: PARSE וַתְּהִי (See §12.6.2) *Q imf w 3f s >* לבן

Q17: Why is this verb feminine? *because the word 'brick' is feminine*

Genesis 11.4

וַיֹּאמְרוּ הָבָה נִבְנֶה־לָּנוּ עִיר וּמִגְדָּל

Q18: What is the ה ending on נִבְנֶה? *part of the verb root* בנה

Q19: PARSE נִבְנֶה (See §12.6.2) *Q imf coh 1c pl >* בנה

Q20: What part of speech is the נו on לָּנוּ? *pronominal suffix 'us'*

וְרֹאשׁוֹ בַשָּׁמַיִם See Williams §494

וְנַעֲשֶׂה־לָּנוּ שֵׁם

Q21: PARSE וְנַעֲשֶׂה *Q imf coh 1c pl >* עשה

פֶּן־נָפוּץ עַל־פְּנֵי כָל־הָאָרֶץ:

Q22: PARSE נָפוּץ *Q imf 1c pl >* פוץ

Q23: How would you form the *nifal* imf 1cp of this verb (See §15.1.3)? נִפּוֹץ

Genesis 11.5

וַיֵּרֶד יְהוָה לִרְאֹת אֶת־הָעִיר וְאֶת־הַמִּגְדָּל

Q24: Is the *tsere* under the י the usual vowel for a *qal* imf? *no, but this verb begins with yod, which assimilates with the yod preformative and causes the chireq to lengthen to a tsere*

Q25: PARSE לִרְאֹת *Q inf cs* > ראה

Q26: Why does לִרְאֹת end with ת? (See §12.6.2) *final* ה *will change to* ת *in the infinitive form*

אֲשֶׁר בָּנוּ בְּנֵי הָאָדָם׃

Q27: PARSE בָּנוּ *Q pf 3c pl* > בנה

Genesis 11.6

וְזֶה הַחִלָּם לַעֲשׂוֹת   (§7.6)

Q28: Why is there a *dagesh* in the ל? (§16.1.2) *to compensate for the assimilation of the* ל *in the verb* חלל

Q29: What stem is indicated by the הַ? *Hifil*

Q30: PARSE הַחִלָּם *Hif inf cs + pronom suffix 3m pl* > חלל

Q31: PARSE לַעֲשׂוֹת (See §12.6.2) *Q inf cs* > עשה

וְעַתָּה לֹא־יִבָּצֵר מֵהֶם כֹּל אֲשֶׁר יָזְמוּ לַעֲשׂוֹת׃

Q32: PARSE יִבָּצֵר *Nif imf w 3m s* > בצר

Q33: What stem is characterized by a *dagesh* in the first radical of the imperfect, with a *qamets* under the same radical? *Nifal*

Q34: PARSE יָזְמוּ (§26.1.1 #39) *Q imf 3m pl* > זמם

Q35: PARSE לַעֲשׂוֹת (See §12.6.2) *Q inf cs* > עשה

Genesis 11.7

הָבָה נֵרְדָה וְנָבְלָה שָׁם שְׂפָתָם Williams §191

Q36: PARSE וְנָבְלָה (See §16.1.3) *Q imf coh 1c pl* > בלל

Q37: What part of speech is the ה ending on הָבָה, נֵרְדָה and וְנָבְלָה? (§6.1) *volitive* ה

Q38: Is the *tsere* under the נ of נֵרְדָה the usual vowel for a *qal* imf? *no, but this verb begins with yod, which assimilates with the nun preformative and causes the chireq to lengthen to a tsere*

Q39: Why does וְנָבְלָה have a *qamets* under the preformative? *because it is a geminate verb, which takes a qamets*

אֲשֶׁר לֹא יִשְׁמְעוּ אִישׁ שְׂפַת רֵעֵהוּ׃ See Williams §132

Q40: PARSE יִשְׁמְעוּ *Q imf 3m pl* > שמע

Genesis 11.8

וַיָּפֶץ יְהוָה אֹתָם מִשָּׁם עַל־פְּנֵי כָל־הָאָרֶץ

Q41: PARSE וַיָּפֶץ *Q imf w 3m s* > פוץ

וַיַּחְדְּלוּ לִבְנֹת הָעִיר׃

Q42: PARSE וַיַּחְדְּלוּ *Q imf w 3m pl* > חדל

Q43: PARSE לִבְנֹת *Q inf cs* > בנה

Q44: What weak verbs end with ת in the infinitive? *final ה verbs*

Genesis 11.9

וּמִשָּׁם הֱפִיצָם יְהוָה עַל־פְּנֵי כָּל־הָאָרֶץ׃

Q45: PARSE הֱפִיצָם *Hif pf 3m s + pron. suffix 3m pl* > פוץ

Q46: What part of speech is the ם on הֱפִיצָם? *pronominal suffix 3m pl*

Q47: What stem is indicated by a prefixed ה and an infixed י? *Hifil*

CHAPTER 17

Exercise 17—Genesis 12.1-13

Genesis 12.1

לֶךְ־לְךָ מֵאַרְצְךָ וּמִמּוֹלַדְתְּךָ וּמִבֵּית אָבִיךָ

Q1: Only two radicals remain on לֵךְ. What is the third radical? *ה – the verb is* הלך

Q2: PARSE לֵךְ *Q imv 2m s* > הלך

Q3: What part of speech is ךָ? *pronominal suffix 2m s*

Q4: Is אָבִיךָ *father* or *fathers*? *'your father'—'your fathers' would be* אֲבֹתֶיךָ

אֶל־הָאָרֶץ אֲשֶׁר אַרְאֶךָּ׃

Q5: What stem is indicated by the *patach* under the preformative? *Hifil*

Q6: What part of speech is ךָ? *pronominal suffix 2m s*

Q7: PARSE אַרְאֶךָּ *H imf 1c s + pron. suffix 2m s* > ראה

Genesis 12.2

וְאֶעֶשְׂךָ לְגוֹי גָּדוֹל

> **Q8:** Is this a *wayyiqtol*?   *no, it is weyiqtol*
>
> **Q9:** PARSE וְאֶעֶשְׂךָ (See §12.6.2) *Q imf coh 1c s + pron. suffix 2m s >* עשׂה
>
> **Q10:** Is this a simple future (*I shall make you*), or a cohortative (*I will make you*)? See §5.1.2. *cohortative because it is the first word in the clause*

וַאֲבָרֶכְךָ וַאֲגַדְּלָה שְׁמֶךָ וֶהְיֵה בְּרָכָה:

> **Q11:** Piel requires a *dagesh* in the middle radical, so why is there no *dagesh* in the *resh*?   *because resh is a guttural letter*
>
> **Q12:** PARSE וַאֲבָרֶכְךָ   *Piel imf coh 1c s + pron. suffix 2m s >* ברך
>
> **Q13:** What is the ה on וַאֲגַדְּלָה?   *cohortative* ה
>
> **Q14:** PARSE וַאֲגַדְּלָה *Piel imf coh 1c s >* גדל
>
> **Q15:** Are these two verbs (וַאֲבָרֶכְךָ וַאֲגַדְּלָה) *wayyiqtols*?   *no, they are weyiqtols*

Genesis 12.3

וַאֲבָרֲכָה מְבָרְכֶיךָ וּמְקַלֶּלְךָ אָאֹר

> **Q16:** What is the ה? *cohortative*
>
> **Q17:** PARSE וַאֲבָרֲכָה *Piel imf coh 1c s >* ברך
>
> **Q18:** What form of the verb does the מְ indicate? *participle*
>
> **Q19:** PARSE מְבָרְכֶיךָ (See §14.2.2) *Piel ptc m pl + pron. suffix 2 m s >* ברך
>
> **Q20:** PARSE וּמְקַלֶּלְךָ *Piel ptc m s + pron. suffix 2 m s >* קלל
>
> **Q21:** Why is there a י in מְבָרְכֶיךָ, but not in וּמְקַלֶּלְךָ?   *the first ptc is plural and the second is singular*
>
> **Q22:** PARSE אָאֹר *Q imf 1c s >* ארר

וְנִבְרְכוּ בְךָ כֹּל מִשְׁפְּחֹת הָאֲדָמָה:

> **Q23:** What stem is suggested by נִ? (See §14.2.2)   *Nifal*
>
> **Q24:** What part of speech is וּ?   *plural ending*
>
> **Q25:** PARSE וְנִבְרְכוּ *Nif pf 3c pl >* ברך   *weqatal*

Genesis 12.4

וַיֵּלֶךְ אַבְרָם כַּאֲשֶׁר דִּבֶּר אֵלָיו יְהוָה

> **Q26:** Is this a *wayyiqtol*? *yes*
>
> **Q27:** PARSE וַיֵּלֶךְ (See §17.1.3) *Q imf 3m s >* הלך
>
> **Q28:** PARSE דִּבֶּר *Piel pf 3m s >* דבר

וַיֵּלֶךְ אִתּוֹ לוֹט

Q29: What is the difference between אִתּוֹ and אֹתוֹ? אִתּוֹ *is the preposition 'with' and the pronom. suffix attached, whil* אֹתוֹ *is the objective pronoun 'he'*

בְּצֵאתוֹ מֵחָרָן:

Q30: What are the only two forms of the verb to which a prep. may be attached? *infinitive and participle*

Q31: Does this word begin a temporal clause? (§6.5.2) *yes*

Q32: PARSE בְּצֵאתוֹ (See §17.1.5) *Q inf cs + prep. prefix and pron. suffix >* יצא

Genesis 12.5

וַיִּקַּח אַבְרָם אֶת־שָׂרַי אִשְׁתּוֹ

Q33: Why is there a *dagesh* in the ק? (See §14.1.1) *to compensate for the assimilation of the first root letter* ל

Q34: PARSE וַיִּקַּח *Q imf w 3m s >* לקח

וְאֶת־כָּל־רְכוּשָׁם אֲשֶׁר רָכָשׁוּ

Q35: Into what English tense would you translate רָכָשׁוּ? *past perfect 'had acquired', because the action of acquiring happened previous to the main verb in the sentence, 'took'*

Q36: PARSE רָכָשׁוּ *Q pf 3c pl >* רכשׁ

וְאֶת־הַנֶּפֶשׁ אֲשֶׁר־עָשׂוּ בְחָרָן

Q37: PARSE עָשׂוּ (See §12.6.2) *Q pf 3c pl >* עשׂה

Is הַנֶּפֶשׁ singular or plural? *Grammatically it is singular, but it seems to function here like a collective noun.*

וַיֵּצְאוּ לָלֶכֶת אַרְצָה כְּנַעַן

Q38: Why is there a *tsere* under the יְ? (See §17.1.5) *to compensate for the assimilation of the yod*

Q39: PARSE וַיֵּצְאוּ *Q imf w 3m pl >* יצא

Q40: PARSE לָלֶכֶת *Q inf cs >* הלך

Q41: What is the ה on אַרְצָה? (§7.5) *locative, directive* ה

וַיָּבֹאוּ אַרְצָה כְּנַעַן:

Q42: Hollow verbs retain the middle radical in the imperfect. If וַיָּבֹאוּ is imf., why does it not have the middle radical? *the middle radical is lost in the wayyiqtol*

Q43: PARSE וַיָּבֹאוּ (See §15.1.3) *Q imf w 3m pl >* בּוֹא

Genesis 12.6

וַיַּעֲבֹר אַבְרָם בָּאָרֶץ עַד מְקוֹם שְׁכֶם עַד אֵלוֹן מוֹרֶה

Q44: Why is there a *patach* under the י in וַיַּעֲבֹר? *because the verb begins with a guttural letter*

Q45: Classify the construct–genitive phrase אֵלוֹן מוֹרֶה according to §5.3.3. *genitive of specification, location.*

Genesis 12.7

וַיֵּרָא יְהוָה אֶל־אַבְרָם

Q46: וַיֵּרָא How do you know that this is *nifal*? *the qamets under the first root letter of the imperfect, coupled with the tsere under the preformative, which compensates for the dagesh that cannot appear in the guttural resh*

Q47: PARSE וַיֵּרָא (See §12.6.2) *Nif imf w 3m s* > ראה

the final ה *is dropped in the wayyiqtol*

וַיֹּאמֶר לְזַרְעֲךָ אֶתֵּן אֶת־הָאָרֶץ הַזֹּאת

Q48: PARSE אֶתֵּן (See §14.1.2) *Q imf 1c s* > נתן

וַיִּבֶן שָׁם מִזְבֵּחַ לַיהוָה הַנִּרְאֶה אֵלָיו:

Q49: וַיִּבֶן What is the third radical? *the final* ה *is dropped in the wayyiqtol*

Q50: PARSE וַיִּבֶן (See §12.6.2) *Q imf w 3m s* > נתן

Q51: הַנִּרְאֶה What part of speech is the ה? *definite article*

Q52: PARSE הַנִּרְאֶה (See §12.6.2) *Nif ptc m s* > ראה

Genesis 12.8

וַיַּעְתֵּק מִשָּׁם הָהָרָה מִקֶּדֶם לְבֵית־אֵל

Q53: PARSE וַיַּעְתֵּק (See §13.1.2) *Hif imf w 3m s* > עתק

וַיֵּט אָהֳלֹה בֵּית־אֵל מִיָּם וְהָעַי מִקֶּדֶם

Q54: וַיֵּט Two radicals are missing, what are they? נ *and* ה

Q55: PARSE וַיֵּט *Q imf w 3m s* > נטה

וַיִּבֶן־שָׁם מִזְבֵּחַ לַיהוָה וַיִּקְרָא בְּשֵׁם יְהוָה:

Q56: וַיִּבֶן What third radical is dropped from the *wayyiqtol*? ה

Q57: PARSE וַיִּבֶן (See §12.6.2) *Q imf w 3m s* > בנה

Genesis 12.9

וַיִּסַּע אַבְרָם הָלוֹךְ וְנָסוֹעַ הַנֶּגְבָּה:

Q58: PARSE וַיִּסַּע *Q imf w 3m s* > נסע

Q59: PARSE הָלוֹךְ *Q inf absolute* > הלך

62

Q60: PARSE וְנָסוֹעַ *Q inf absolute + prefixed* ו < נסע

Genesis 12.10

וַיֵּרֶד אַבְרָם מִצְרַיְמָה לָגוּר שָׁם

    Q61: PARSE וַיֵּרֶד (See §17.1.5) *Q imf w 3m s* < ירד

    Q62: PARSE לָגוּר (See §15.1.3) *Q inf cs* < גור

Genesis 12.11

וַיְהִי כַּאֲשֶׁר הִקְרִיב לָבוֹא מִצְרָיְמָה

    Q63: PARSE הִקְרִיב *Hif pf 3m s* < קרב

    Q64: PARSE לָבוֹא (See §15.1.3) *Q inf cs* < בוא

וַיֹּאמֶר אֶל־שָׂרַי אִשְׁתּוֹ

הִנֵּה־נָא יָדַעְתִּי כִּי אִשָּׁה יְפַת־מַרְאֶה אָתְּ:

    Q65: PARSE יָדַעְתִּי *Q pf 1c s* < ידע

Genesis 12.12

(§26.1.1 #41) וְהָיָה כִּי־יִרְאוּ אֹתָךְ הַמִּצְרִים

    Q66: PARSE יִרְאוּ (See §12.6.2) *Q imf 3m pl* < ראה

(§26.1.1 #47) וְאָמְרוּ אִשְׁתּוֹ זֹאת וְהָרְגוּ אֹתִי וְאֹתָךְ יְחַיּוּ:

    Q67: PARSE וְהָרְגוּ *Q pf 3c pl weqatal* < הרג

    Q68: PARSE יְחַיּוּ (See §12.6.2) *Piel imf 3m pl* < חיה

Genesis 12.13

אִמְרִי־נָא אֲחֹתִי אָתְּ

    Q69: PARSE אִמְרִי *Q imv 2f s* < אמר

לְמַעַן יִיטַב־לִי בַעֲבוּרֵךְ

    Q70: PARSE יִיטַב *Q imf 3m s* < יטב

וְחָיְתָה נַפְשִׁי בִּגְלָלֵךְ:

    Q71: PARSE וְחָיְתָה *Q pf 3f s weqatal* < חיה

CHAPTER 18

Exercise 18—Genesis 22.1-14

Genesis 22.1

וַיְהִי אַחַר הַדְּבָרִים הָאֵלֶּה וְהָאֱלֹהִים נִסָּה אֶת־אַבְרָהָם

Q1: Should the *vav* on הָאֱלֹהִים be translated 1) *and*, 2) *but*, or 3) *that*?

'that', because it follows an introductory temporal clause

Q2: Why is there a *dagesh* in נִסָּה? *it is Piel*

Q3: Why is the last vowel of נִסָּה a *qamets* instead of *tsere*? *because of the final* ה

Q4: PARSE נִסָּה *Piel pf 3m s >* נסה

וַיֹּאמֶר אֵלָיו אַבְרָהָם וַיֹּאמֶר הִנֵּנִי:

Q5: Does the accent above אֵלָיו indicate pause or continuation? *pause*

Q6: What is the name of the accent mark? *zaqqef*

Genesis 22.2

וַיֹּאמֶר קַח־נָא אֶת־בִּנְךָ אֶת־יְחִידְךָ

Q7: What is the missing radical in קַח? (§14.1.1) *the first radical,* ל

Q8: Is this a geminate verb? *no*

Q9: PARSE קַח *Q imv 2m s >* לקח

Q10: What part of speech is ךָ on בִּנְךָ? *pronominal suffix 2m s, 'you'*

אֲשֶׁר־אָהַבְתָּ אֶת־יִצְחָק

Q11: PARSE אָהַבְתָּ *Q pf 2m s >* אהב

Q12: Into what tense should we translate אָהַבְתָּ? *present tense because actions and emotions that began in the past and are continued into the present are translated as present tense, e.g. love, hate, know*

וְלֶךְ־לְךָ אֶל־אֶרֶץ הַמֹּרִיָּה

Q13: PARSE וְלֶךְ *Q imv 2m s + conj. >* הלך

וְהַעֲלֵהוּ שָׁם לְעֹלָה עַל אַחַד הֶהָרִים (§26.1.1 #62)

Q14: What stem has a prefixed הַ? *Hifil, this is an imperative + 3m s suffix*

אֲשֶׁר אֹמַר אֵלֶיךָ:

Q15: PARSE אֹמַר *Q imf 1c s >* אמר *the alef has assimilated*

Q16: Into what tense should we translate אֹמַר? *future because it is an imperfect following the relative pronoun 'which'*

64

Genesis 22.3

וַיַּשְׁכֵּם אַבְרָהָם בַּבֹּקֶר

> **Q17:** What stem is indicated by the *patach* under the preformative יְ? *Hifil*

> **Q18:** PARSE וַיַּשְׁכֵּם *Hifil imf w 3m s >* שׁכם

וַיַּחֲבֹשׁ אֶת־חֲמֹרוֹ

> **Q19:** Is וַיַּחֲבֹשׁ hifil? Why or why not? *No, because there is no e-class verb (tsere, chiriq, or segol) after the second root letter; the cholem is standard for Qal imperfect and the patach under the preformative is due to the guttural letter*

> **Q20:** PARSE וַיַּחֲבֹשׁ *Q imf w 3m s >* חבש

וַיִּקַּח אֶת־שְׁנֵי נְעָרָיו אִתּוֹ וְאֵת יִצְחָק בְּנוֹ

> **Q21:** Why is there a *dagesh* in the ק of וַיִּקַּח? *to compensate for the assimilation of the first root letter,* ל

> **Q22:** PARSE וַיִּקַּח *Q imf w 3m s >* לקח

וַיְבַקַּע עֲצֵי עֹלָה

> **Q23:** What stem is suggested by the *sheva* under the preformative in וַיְבַקַּע? *Piel*

> **Q24:** What stem is suggested by the *dagesh* in the ק of וַיְבַקַּע? *Piel*

> **Q25:** Classify the construct–genitive עֲצֵי עֹלָה according to §5.3.3. *Adverbial genitive of goal or purpose.*

וַיָּקָם וַיֵּלֶךְ אֶל־הַמָּקוֹם אֲשֶׁר־אָמַר־לוֹ הָאֱלֹהִים:

> **Q26:** What two weak verb patterns have *qamets* under the preformative of the imperfect? *hollow verbs and geminate verbs*

> **Q27:** PARSE וַיָּקָם *Q imf w 3m s >* קום

> **Q28:** What weak verb pattern is characterized by *tsere* under the preformative of the imperfect? *initial yod verbs and the verb* הלך

> **Q29:** PARSE וַיֵּלֶךְ *Q imf w 3m s >* הלך

Genesis 22.4

בַּיּוֹם הַשְּׁלִישִׁי וַיִּשָּׂא אַבְרָהָם אֶת־עֵינָיו

> **Q30:** Why is there a *dagesh* in the שׂ of וַיִּשָּׂא? *to compensate for the assimilation of the letter nun*

> **Q31:** PARSE וַיִּשָּׂא *Q imf w 3m s >* נשא

וַיַּרְא אֶת־הַמָּקוֹם מֵרָחֹק:

> **Q32:** PARSE וַיַּרְא *Q imf w 3m s >* ראה

Genesis 22.5

וַיֹּאמֶר אַבְרָהָם אֶל־נְעָרָיו שְׁבוּ־לָכֶם פֹּה עִם־הַחֲמוֹר

Q33: PARSE שְׁבוּ   *Q imv 2m pl >* יָשׁב

וַאֲנִי וְהַנַּעַר נֵלְכָה עַד־כֹּה

Q34: What part of speech is the ה on the end of נֵלְכָה? *volitive* ה

Q35: PARSE נֵלְכָה   *Q imf coh 1c pl >* הָלַךְ

וְנִשְׁתַּחֲוֶה וְנָשׁוּבָה אֲלֵיכֶם:

Q36: What tense is וְנִשְׁתַּחֲוֶה? *future, weyiqtol cohortative*

Q37: PARSE וְנִשְׁתַּחֲוֶה   *Hishtafel imf 1c pl >* חוה

Q38: What part of speech is the ה on וְנָשׁוּבָה? *volitive* ה

Q39: PARSE וְנָשׁוּבָה   *Q imf coh 1c pl >* שׁוּב

Genesis 22.6

וַיִּקַּח אַבְרָהָם אֶת־עֲצֵי הָעֹלָה

Q40: PARSE וַיִּקַּח   *Q imf w 3m s >* לָקַח

וַיָּשֶׂם עַל־יִצְחָק בְּנוֹ

Q41: What weak verb pattern is suggested by the *qamets* in וַיָּשֶׂם? *hollow verb*

Q42: PARSE וַיָּשֶׂם   *Q imf w 3m s >* שִׂים

וַיֵּלְכוּ שְׁנֵיהֶם יַחְדָּו:

Q43: PARSE וַיֵּלְכוּ   *Q imf w 3m pl >* הָלַךְ (§22.13)

Genesis 22.8

וַיֹּאמֶר אַבְרָהָם אֱלֹהִים יִרְאֶה־לּוֹ הַשֶּׂה לְעֹלָה בְּנִי

Q44: Into what tense should we translate יִרְאֶה? *future tense, yiqtol*

Q45: PARSE יִרְאֶה   *Q imf 3m s >* רָאה

וַיֵּלְכוּ שְׁנֵיהֶם יַחְדָּו:

Q46: PARSE וַיֵּלְכוּ   *Q imf w 3m pl >* הָלַךְ

Genesis 22.9

וַיָּבֹאוּ אֶל־הַמָּקוֹם אֲשֶׁר אָמַר־לוֹ הָאֱלֹהִים

Q47: PARSE וַיָּבֹאוּ   *Q imf w 3m pl >* בּוֹא

Q48: Into what tense should we translate אָמַר? *past perfect, because the action of the verb 'he had said' occurred before the main verb of the sentence, 'they came'*

וַיִּבֶן שָׁם אַבְרָהָם אֶת־הַמִּזְבֵּחַ

> **Q49:** What root letter is usually dropped from the *wayyiqtol*, as in וַיִּבֶן? ה (§12.6.2)

> **Q50:** PARSE וַיִּבֶן   *Q imf w 3m s >* בנה

וַיַּעֲרֹךְ אֶת־הָעֵצִים וַיַּעֲקֹד אֶת־יִצְחָק בְּנוֹ

> **Q51:** Why is there a *patach* under the preformative in וַיַּעֲרֹךְ? *the first root letter is a guttural*

> **Q52:** PARSE וַיַּעֲרֹךְ   *Q imf w 3m s >* ערך

> PARSE וַיַּעֲקֹד   *Q imf w 3m s >* עקד

וַיָּשֶׂם אֹתוֹ עַל־הַמִּזְבֵּחַ מִמַּעַל לָעֵצִים:

> **Q53:** Why does the preformative of וַיָּשֶׂם have *qamets*? *because this is a hollow verb*

> **Q54:** PARSE וַיָּשֶׂם   *Q imf w 3m s >* שִׂים

Genesis 22.10

וַיִּשְׁלַח אַבְרָהָם אֶת־יָדוֹ

> **Q55:** Why is there a *patach* under the ל of וַיִּשְׁלַח? *because the final root letter is a guttural*

> **Q56:** PARSE וַיִּשְׁלַח   *Q imf w 3m s >* שלח

וַיִּקַּח אֶת־הַמַּאֲכֶלֶת לִשְׁחֹט אֶת־בְּנוֹ:

> **Q57:** What radical is missing from וַיִּקַּח? *the first letter,* ל

> **Q58:** PARSE וַיִּקַּח   *Q imf w 3m s >* לקח

> **Q59:** What verb form is usually indicated by a prefixed ל? *infinitive construct*

> **Q60:** PARSE לִשְׁחֹט   *Q inf cs >* שחט

Genesis 22.11

וַיִּקְרָא אֵלָיו מַלְאַךְ יְהוָה מִן־הַשָּׁמַיִם

> **Q61:** PARSE וַיִּקְרָא   *Q imf w 3m s >* קרא

Genesis 22.12

וַיֹּאמֶר אַל־תִּשְׁלַח יָדְךָ אֶל־הַנַּעַר

> **Q62:** PARSE תִּשְׁלַח   *Q imf jussive 2m s >* שלח

וְאַל־תַּעַשׂ לוֹ מְאוּמָה

> **Q63:** PARSE תַּעַשׂ   *Q imf jussive 2m s >* עשה

כִּי עַתָּה יָדַעְתִּי כִּי־יְרֵא אֱלֹהִים אַתָּה

Q64: PARSE יָדַעְתִּי   *Q pf 1c s* > ידע

Q65: Is יְרֵא a ptc. or adj.? *grammatically, the forms of the adjective and the participle in the construct state would be identical.* Word order suggests that יְרֵא is in the construct state, and the phrase means *a fearer of God* (see §5.3).

וְלֹא חָשַׂכְתָּ אֶת־בִּנְךָ אֶת־יְחִידְךָ מִמֶּנִּי:

Q66: PARSE חָשַׂכְתָּ   *Q pf 2m s* > חשׂך

Q67: What tense is חָשַׂכְתָּ? *past tense*

Genesis 22.13

וַיִּשָּׂא אַבְרָהָם אֶת־עֵינָיו וַיַּרְא

Q68: PARSE וַיִּשָּׂא   *Q imf w 3m s* > נשׂא

Q69: PARSE וַיַּרְא   *Q imf w 3m s* > ראה

וְהִנֵּה־אַיִל אַחַר נֶאֱחַז בַּסְּבַךְ בְּקַרְנָיו

Q70: PARSE נֶאֱחַז   *Nif pf 3m s* > אחז

וַיֵּלֶךְ אַבְרָהָם וַיִּקַּח אֶת־הָאַיִל

Q71: PARSE וַיֵּלֶךְ   *Q imf w 3m s* > הלך

Q72: PARSE וַיִּקַּח   *Q imf w 3m s* > לקח

וַיַּעֲלֵהוּ לְעֹלָה תַּחַת בְּנוֹ:

Q73: PARSE וַיַּעֲלֵהוּ   *Hif imf w 3m s + pron. suffix 3m s* > עלה

Genesis 22.14

אֲשֶׁר יֵאָמֵר הַיּוֹם בְּהַר יְהוָה יֵרָאֶה:

Q74: PARSE יֵאָמֵר   *Nif imf 3m s* > אמר

Q75: PARSE יֵרָאֶה   *Nif imf 3m s* > ראה

Chapter 19

Exercise 19—Genesis 37.1-18

Genesis 37.1

וַיֵּשֶׁב יַעֲקֹב בְּאֶרֶץ מְגוּרֵי אָבִיו בְּאֶרֶץ כְּנָעַן:

Q1: What weak verb pattern is indicated by the *tsere* under the preformative in the verb וַיֵּשֶׁב? *initial yod verbs*

Q2: PARSE וַיֵּשֶׁב   *Q imf w 3m s* > ישׁב

Q3: What would the root be if the spelling had been וַיֵּשֶׁב? שׁוּב

Q4: Is מְגוּרֵי a definite noun? If so, why does it not have the article? *it is in construct with 'his father', who is a definite person, therefore the entire phrase, 'sojournings of his father', is definite even without the article*

Q5: Is אָבִיו *his father* or *his fathers*? *'his father'—'his fathers' would be* אֲבֹתָיו

Genesis 37.2

אֵלֶּה תֹּלְדוֹת יַעֲקֹב

Q6: Could אֵלֶּה תֹּלְדוֹת be translated *these generations*? *no, because the attributive adjective usually follows the noun and would normally have the article—the phrase 'these days' would be* הַתֹּלְדוֹת הָאֵלֶּה

Q7: This is a verbless clause; what is its syntactical function? *as an introductory heading for a new story*

יוֹסֵף בֶּן־שְׁבַע־עֶשְׂרֵה שָׁנָה הָיָה רֹעֶה אֶת־אֶחָיו בַּצֹּאן

Q8: Is שָׁנָה singular or plural? *singular, but idiomatically represents the plural, similar to the English 'an eight foot board'*

Q9: PARSE הָיָה *Q pf 3m s >* היה

Q10: Does the perfect suggest the beginning of a new narrative? *yes*

Q11: Is רֹעֶה a ptc. or a noun? *the ptc. and noun have the same form; in this case the translation is not clear, either it is 'he was a shepherd with his brothers among the flock' or 'he was shepherding with his brothers among the flock'*

Q12: How do you translate אֶת? *with*

וְהוּא נַעַר אֶת־בְּנֵי בִלְהָה וְאֶת־בְּנֵי זִלְפָּה נְשֵׁי אָבִיו

Q13: This sentence begins with a *vav* attached to a pronoun. Therefore, is the sentence sequential or non-sequential with the previous clause? *it is contemporaneous with the previous clause, therefore non-sequential*

וַיָּבֵא יוֹסֵף אֶת־דִּבָּתָם רָעָה אֶל־אֲבִיהֶם:

Q14: What weak verb patterns are suggested by the *qamets* under the preformative of וַיָּבֵא? *hollow verb, geminate verb, Hifil*

Q15: PARSE וַיָּבֵא *Hif imf w 3m s >* בוֹא

Q16: What stem is suggested by the *tsere*? *Hifil*

Q17: What part of speech is ם on דִּבָּתָם? *pronominal suffix 3m pl*

Q18: What part of speech is the הֶם on אֲבִיהֶם? *pronominal suffix 3m pl*

Genesis 37.3

וְיִשְׂרָאֵל אָהַב אֶת־יוֹסֵף מִכָּל־בָּנָיו

Q19: Is the action of this clause subsequent to the action of the previous clause, or is it contemporaneous? *contemporaneous, background information*

Q20: PARSE אָהַב   *Q pf 3m s* > אהב

וְעָשָׂה לֹו כְּתֹנֶת פַּסִּים:

Q21: PARSE וְעָשָׂה   *Q pf weqatal 3m s* > עשׂה

Genesis 37.4

וַיִּרְאוּ אֶחָיו כִּי־אֹתֹו אָהַב אֲבִיהֶם מִכָּל־אֶחָיו

Q22: What radical is missing from וַיִּרְאוּ? ה

Q23: PARSE וַיִּרְאוּ   *Q imf w 3m pl* > ראה

Q24: Is אֹתֹו in an emphatic position? *yes*

וַיִּשְׂנְאוּ אֹתֹו וְלֹא יָכְלוּ דַּבְּרֹו לְשָׁלֹם:

Q25: PARSE וַיִּשְׂנְאוּ   *Q imf w 3m pl* > ישׂב

Q26: PARSE יָכְלוּ   *Q pf 3c pl* > יכל

Q27: PARSE דַּבְּרֹו   *Piel inf cs + pron. suffix 3m s* > הבר

Genesis 37.5

וַיַּחֲלֹם יֹוסֵף חֲלֹום וַיַּגֵּד לְאֶחָיו

Q28: Why is there a *dagesh* in the ג of וַיַּגֵּד? *to compensate for the assimilation of the letter nun; the root verb is* נגד

Q29: What stem is suggested by the *patach* under the preformative of וַיַּגֵּד (note also the *tsere*)? *Hifil*

Q30: PARSE וַיַּגֵּד   *Hif imf w 3m s* > נגד

וַיֹּוסִפוּ עֹוד שְׂנֹא אֹתֹו:

Q31: What is the only stem that has ֹו following the imperfect preformative? *Hifil*

Q32: PARSE וַיֹּוסִפוּ   *Hif imf w 3m pl* > יסף

Q33: PARSE שְׂנֹא   *Q inf cs* > שׂנא

Q34: What verb form is characterized by the *cholem* after the second root letter? *infinitives*

Genesis 37.6

וַיֹּאמֶר אֲלֵיהֶם שִׁמְעוּ־נָא הַחֲלֹום הַזֶּה אֲשֶׁר חָלָמְתִּי:

Q35: PARSE שִׁמְעוּ   *Q imv 2m pl* > שׁמע

Q36: PARSE חָלָמְתִּי   *Q pf 1c s* > חלם

Genesis 37.7

וְהִנֵּה אֲנַחְנוּ מְאַלְּמִים אֲלֻמִּים בְּתוֹךְ הַשָּׂדֶה

> **Q37:** What verb form and stem is characterized by מְ? *Piel participle*
>
> How does this ptc. function in the sentence? *background information*

וְהִנֵּה קָמָה אֲלֻמָּתִי וְגַם־נִצָּבָה

> **Q38:** What part of speech is the ה on קָמָה? *feminine singular sufformative of the perfect*
>
> **Q39:** PARSE קָמָה *Q pf 3f s* > קום
>
> **Q40:** PARSE נִצָּבָה *Nif pf 3c s* > נצב

וְהִנֵּה תְסֻבֶּינָה אֲלֻמֹּתֵיכֶם וַתִּשְׁתַּחֲוֶיןָ לַאֲלֻמָּתִי:

> **Q41:** PARSE תְסֻבֶּינָה *Q imf 3f pl* > סבב
>
> See Holladay, *Lexicon*, p. 251-52, *polel*. Is ֶיןָ the same morpheme as ־נָה? *yes*
>
> **Q42:** PARSE וַתִּשְׁתַּחֲוֶיןָ *Q imf w 3f pl* > חוה

Genesis 37.8

וַיֹּאמְרוּ לוֹ אֶחָיו הֲמָלֹךְ תִּמְלֹךְ עָלֵינוּ

> **Q43:** What is the הֲ on הֲמָלֹךְ? (§12.7) *interrogative particle*
>
> **Q44:** What verb forms are characterized by the *cholem* after the second root letter? (§5.1 and §6.5) *imperfect, imperative, and infinitive*
>
> **Q45:** PARSE הֲמָלֹךְ *Q infin absolute* > מלך
>
> **Q46:** PARSE תִּמְלֹךְ *Q imf 2m s* > מלך

אִם־מָשׁוֹל תִּמְשֹׁל בָּנוּ

> **Q47:** PARSE מָשׁוֹל *Q infin absolute* > משל
>
> **Q48:** PARSE תִּמְשֹׁל *Q imf 2m s* > משל

וַיּוֹסִפוּ עוֹד שְׂנֹא אֹתוֹ עַל־חֲלֹמֹתָיו וְעַל־דְּבָרָיו: (Repeated, cf. v. 5)

> **Q49:** What stem has ו following the imperfect preformative? (§17.1.5) *Hifil*
>
> **Q50:** PARSE וַיּוֹסִפוּ *Hif imf w 3m pl* > יסף

Genesis 37.9

וַיַּחֲלֹם עוֹד חֲלוֹם אַחֵר וַיְסַפֵּר אֹתוֹ לְאֶחָיו

> **Q51:** PARSE וַיְסַפֵּר *Piel imf w 3m s* > ספר
>
> **Q52:** What stem is characterized by *sheva* under the imperfect preformative? *Piel*

וַיֹּאמֶר הִנֵּה חָלַמְתִּי חֲלוֹם עוֹד

וְהִנֵּה הַשֶּׁמֶשׁ וְהַיָּרֵחַ וְאַחַד עָשָׂר כּוֹכָבִים מִשְׁתַּחֲוִים לִי׃

Q53: PARSE מִשְׁתַּחֲוִים *Histafel ptc m pl* > חוה

Genesis 37.10

וַיְסַפֵּר אֶל־אָבִיו וְאֶל־אֶחָיו
וַיִּגְעַר־בּוֹ אָבִיו וַיֹּאמֶר לוֹ

Q54: PARSE וַיִּגְעַר *Q imf w 3m s* > גער

מָה הַחֲלוֹם הַזֶּה אֲשֶׁר חָלָמְתָּ

Q55: PARSE חָלָמְתָּ *Q pf 3c pl* > כל

הֲבוֹא נָבוֹא אֲנִי וְאִמְּךָ וְאַחֶיךָ לְהִשְׁתַּחֲוֹת לְךָ אָרְצָה׃

Q56: PARSE הֲבוֹא

Q57: What part of speech is the הֲ prefix? (§12.7.) *interrogative particle*

Q58: PARSE נָבוֹא *Q imf 2c pl* > בוֹא

Q59: PARSE לְהִשְׁתַּחֲוֹת *Histafel infin cs* > חוה

Genesis 37.11

וַיְקַנְאוּ־בוֹ אֶחָיו וְאָבִיו שָׁמַר אֶת־הַדָּבָר׃

Q60: PARSE וַיְקַנְאוּ *Piel imf w 3m pl* > קנא

Q61: What stem is indicated by the *sheva* under the preformative? *Piel*

Genesis 37.12

וַיֵּלְכוּ אֶחָיו לִרְעוֹת אֶת־צֹאן אֲבִיהֶם בִּשְׁכֶם׃

Q62: PARSE וַיֵּלְכוּ *Q imf w 3m pl* > הלך

Q63: PARSE לִרְעוֹת *Q inf cs* > רעה

Genesis 37.13

וַיֹּאמֶר יִשְׂרָאֵל אֶל־יוֹסֵף
הֲלוֹא אַחֶיךָ רֹעִים בִּשְׁכֶם

Q64: What part of speech is the הֲ on הֲלוֹא? (§12.7.) *interrogative particle*

לְכָה וְאֶשְׁלָחֲךָ אֲלֵיהֶם וַיֹּאמֶר לוֹ הִנֵּנִי׃

Q65: PARSE לְכָה *Q imv 2m s* > הלך

Q66: What part of speech is the ה on לְכָה? (§6.2) *volitive* ה

Genesis 37.14

וְאֶת־שְׁלוֹם הַצֹּאן

    Q67: PARSE לֵךְ   *Q imv 2m s* > הלך

    Q68: PARSE רְאֵה   *Q imv 2m s* > ראה

וַהֲשִׁבֵנִי דָּבָר

    Q69: PARSE וַהֲשִׁבֵנִי   *Hif imv 2m s* > שׁוב   *prefixed vav and pron. suffix 1c s*

וַיִּשְׁלָחֵהוּ מֵעֵמֶק חֶבְרוֹן וַיָּבֹא שְׁכֶמָה:

    Q70: PARSE וַיִּשְׁלָחֵהוּ   *Q imf w 3m s* > שׁלח

    Q71: What part of speech is the הו suffix on וַיִּשְׁלָחֵהוּ? *pronominal suffix 3m s*

    Q72: PARSE וַיָּבֹא   *Q imf w 3m s* > בוא

    Q73: What part of speech is the ה on שְׁכֶמָה? *locative, directional* ה

Genesis 37.15

וַיִּמְצָאֵהוּ אִישׁ וְהִנֵּה תֹעֶה בַּשָּׂדֶה

    Q74: PARSE תֹעֶה   *Q ptc m s* > תעה

Genesis 37.16

הַגִּידָה־נָּא לִי אֵיפֹה הֵם רֹעִים:

    Q75: PARSE הַגִּידָה   *Hif imv 2m s* > נגד

Genesis 37.17

וַיֹּאמֶר הָאִישׁ נָסְעוּ מִזֶּה

    Q76: PARSE נָסְעוּ   *Q pf 3c pl* > נסע

כִּי שָׁמַעְתִּי אֹמְרִים נֵלְכָה דֹּתָיְנָה

    Q77: PARSE נֵלְכָה   *Q imf coh 1c pl* > הלך

וַיֵּלֶךְ יוֹסֵף אַחַר אֶחָיו וַיִּמְצָאֵם בְּדֹתָן:

    Q78: PARSE וַיִּמְצָאֵם   *Q imf w 3m s + pron. suffix 3m pl* > שׁב

Genesis 37.18

וַיִּרְאוּ אֹתוֹ מֵרָחֹק וּבְטֶרֶם יִקְרַב אֲלֵיהֶם

    Q79: PARSE וַיִּרְאוּ   *Q imf w 3m pl* > ראה

וַיִּתְנַכְּלוּ אֹתוֹ לַהֲמִיתוֹ:

    Q80: PARSE וַיִּתְנַכְּלוּ   *Hitpael imf w 3m pl* > נכל

    Q81: PARSE לַהֲמִיתוֹ   *Hifil inf cs + pron. suffix 3m s* > מות

Printed in Great Britain
by Amazon

59842909R00047